全国高等教育商务英语规划系列教材

商务英语翻译
Business English Translation

主　编　金焕荣
副主编　孙志祥
编　者　金焕荣　刘　萱　季甜甜

苏州大学出版社

图书在版编目(CIP)数据

商务英语翻译 = Business English Translation / 金焕荣主编. —苏州:苏州大学出版社,2022.1
全国高等教育商务英语规划系列教材
ISBN 978-7-5672-3818-3

Ⅰ.①商… Ⅱ.①金… Ⅲ.①商务-英语-翻译-高等学校-教材 Ⅳ.①H315.9

中国版本图书馆 CIP 数据核字(2022)第 001574 号

书　　名:	商务英语翻译
	Business English Translation
主　　编:	金焕荣
策划编辑:	汤定军
责任编辑:	汤定军
装帧设计:	吴　钰
出版发行:	苏州大学出版社(Soochow University Press)
社　　址:	苏州市十梓街1号　邮编:215006
印　　刷:	江苏凤凰数码印务有限公司
邮购热线:	0512-67480030
销售热线:	0512-67481020
开　　本:	787 mm×1 092 mm　1/16　印张:10.75　字数:255 千
版　　次:	2022 年 1 月第 1 版
印　　次:	2022 年 1 月第 1 次印刷
书　　号:	ISBN 978-7-5672-3818-3
定　　价:	36.00 元

凡购本社图书发现印装错误,请与本社联系调换。服务热线:0512-67481020

苏州大学出版社营销部　电话:0512-67481020
苏州大学出版社网址　http://www.sudapress.com
苏州大学出版社邮箱　sdcbs@suda.edu.cn

全国高等教育商务英语规划系列教材

顾 问	徐青根　鲁加升

编　委　（以姓氏笔画为序）

于延梅　王红华　王金华　王　娅
王　翔　王德丽　毛卫强　方小勇
文　格　朱冬梅　刘　萱　孙亚玲
孙志祥　李卫东　步阳辉　季甜甜
季　宇　张　莹　张夏菲　张　涛
陈东东　陈　羔　陈　培　林又佳
杨　晓　金焕荣　郑　骏　顾　红
顾秀梅　顾　薇　袁海燕　施　翔
姚春宁　姚菊霞　徐　健　徐　源
程进军　曾　艳　潘　珺　穆连涛

策　划　汤定军

编者的话

21世纪的中国，改革开放不断深化，对外经济交往愈加频繁。在经济全球化的大背景下，许多外国企业相继来华投资，我国许多企业也力争打入国际市场，以谋求更大的发展。目前，我国的对外经济交流已发展到对外贸易、对外投资、对外经济技术合作等多个领域。因此，日益广泛的国际商务领域对国际商务英语人才的培养在数量上和质量上都提出了新的要求，而许多涉外用人单位对精通商务英语的求职者的青睐也造成了大专院校及社会上的青年热衷于学习商务英语的景象。翻译是对外交流的工具，所以离开翻译谈交流显然是不可能的。目前，我国的翻译产业正在飞速发展，而随着我国对外开放的深入，商务翻译在整个翻译产业链中占据越来越重要的地位。本教材编写的宗旨一方面是为我国商务翻译人才队伍的发展推波助澜，另一方面也期望能够帮助各类读者在激烈的职场竞争中占据更有利的地位。

选稿之初，编者从两个角度出发：一方面考虑教材的时代性，力求内容新颖，与时俱进；另一方面考虑教材的实用性和科学性，争取涉及广泛，适合翻译。在选稿过程中，编者严格依照以上两个出发点，经过多重考虑，层层筛选，最终选定的文章不仅内容新颖，在相关领域具有代表性，而且篇章完整，有语言点以及翻译重点。这些文章大多出自近年来国内外出版的专著、知名报刊或杂志，也有部分内容来自一些著名经贸类英文网站，内容涉及经济、贸易、金融、投资、营销、管理、商务文化、电子商务、旅游等多个方面。通过学习本教材，学习者不仅可以扩大国际商务知识面，而且能够切实提高翻译能力。

在编写过程中，我们参阅了国内外出版的大量有关资料和信息。主要参考文献目录附于书末。在此，谨表诚挚的谢意。

由于编者经验不足、水平有限，错漏之处在所难免，恳请学界同仁和读者不吝赐教。

金焕荣
2021 年 10 月

使用说明

本书可用作英语专业研究生、本科生及专科生的翻译教材，也可作为已通过国家英语等级考试的经济、贸易、管理等相关专业学生的自学教材或专业英语教材，还可供企业在职人员培训时使用以及有志于从事国际商务活动的人士自学之用。

本书共由18个单元组成，每单元有2篇英译汉、1篇汉译英。英译汉部分首先列出文中重点词汇让学习者提前预习，既能促进学习者自学能力的提高，又可避免学习者在翻译过程中因为词汇欠缺而影响对文章的理解。每篇英文后面都附有注释，这一部分列出了该篇文章翻译中的重点句、难句，不但为这些句子提供了参考译文，还着重讲解了句中重点词汇的用法，解析了适用的翻译方法，并介绍了相关商贸背景知识。本着始终对读者负责的态度，为了力求准确，所有词汇讲解和商务知识介绍都是编者经过仔细查阅专业词典或书籍后做出的。每个单元结尾编者都根据正文有针对性地提供了翻译练习，以帮助学习者更牢固地掌握相关词汇和句型。另外，每两个单元之后都有一个翻译技巧专题讲解，其中介绍了许多实用的翻译方法并提供了大量例句讲解。

本书用作全日制学生的教材时，建议一周开设4个课时，每周讲解一个单元，一学期可将全书内容讲解完毕。由于英译汉部分有些文章难度较大或篇幅较长，教师可酌情选取一篇重点讲解，另一篇供学生自学或进一步探究。

金焕荣
2021年10月

Contents

Unit 1   1

Passage A   International Business Methods（Ⅰ）   1
Passage B   International Business Methods（Ⅱ）   5
Passage C   中国特许经营信息滞后给"假洋品牌"可乘之机   8

Unit 2   9

Passage A   Why Firms Become Multinational Enterprises   9
Passage B   Figuring Out How to Do Business in Japan   12
Passage C   大力实施本土化战略   15
Translation Skills（Ⅰ） 定语从句的翻译   15

Unit 3   18

Passage A   Six Rules of Thumb for Doing Business
            across Cultures   18
Passage B   Managing Corporate Culture   21
Passage C   尽可能使文化冲击最小化   24

Unit 4   26

Passage A   The IMF and the World Bank Today   26
Passage B   Currency Union：A Long-Term Vision?   30
Passage C   通胀与调控   33
Translation Skills（Ⅱ） 被动语态的翻译   33

Unit 5   38

Passage A   Defining Risk   38
Passage B   Risk Adjusted   41
Passage C   投机——让人欲罢不能   44

Unit 6   46

Passage A   An Attempt to Estimate China's Bad Loans Backfires   46
Passage B   China's Reserves: A Money Machine   49
Passage C   采取积极有效措施,促进国际收支基本平衡   51
Translation Skills (Ⅲ)   增词法和减词法   52

Unit 7   56

Passage A   Are Markets Efficient?   56
Passage B   Catching Market Waves   59
Passage C   市场与经济   62

Unit 8   63

Passage A   Strategic Market Management   63
Passage B   Brand Loyalty   66
Passage C   自主品牌:市场的直接交锋   69
Translation Skills (Ⅳ)   翻译中的词性转换   69

Unit 9   72

Passage A   What Is Consumer Behavior?   72
Passage B   Core Values   75
Passage C   贴牌生产   77

Unit 10   79

Passage A   Marketing Strategy   79
Passage B   Managing Innovation   82
Passage C   中西方管理模式的不同   86
Translation Skills (Ⅴ)   长句的翻译   86

Unit 11   89

Passage A   The Manager, the Organization, and the Team   89
Passage B   Leadership, Style, Ethics   92
Passage C   经济全球化对企业人才管理的挑战   95

Unit 12   97

Passage A   Industrial Park Leads Suzhou's Eastward Development   97
Passage B   Action Speaks Louder than Words   100

Passage C 中国经济在世界经济中的作用	104
Translation Skills（Ⅵ） 翻译中的语序调整	104

Unit 13   108

Passage A The Circular Economy Concept	108
Passage B The Awareness Motivating the Circular Economy	111
Passage C 什么是循环经济？	114

Unit 14   115

Passage A Obtaining Scale Economies	115
Passage B Wealth on the Wing	118
Passage C 中国企业海外"本土化"战略	121
Translation Skills（Ⅶ） 翻译中的虚实转换	121

Unit 15   125

Passage A Customizing Your China Wholly Foreign-Owned Enterprises	125
Passage B Integrated Supply Chain Planning	128
Passage C 中国企业融入国际采购链必须克服五大障碍	131

Unit 16   133

Passage A Industry Value Chain Analysis	133
Passage B Outsourcing：Growth by Building on Existing Business	136
Passage C 什么是服务外包？	139
Translation Skills（Ⅷ） 否定句的翻译	140

Unit 17   142

Passage A Electronic B2B in the Auto Industry	142
Passage B Profit Is No Object	145
Passage C C2C 电子商务	148

Unit 18   149

Passage A Inspiring Wine Games	149
Passage B China's Changing Cityscapes	152
Passage C 古老而年轻的苏州	155
Translation Skills（Ⅸ） 数字的翻译	156

Bibliography   158

Unit 1

Passage A (English-Chinese Translation)

International Business Methods (I)
Jeff Madura

Words & Expressions

Work on the following words and expressions and write the translated version in the space provided:

acquisitions of existing operations	_____
foreign subsidiaries	_____
at risk	_____
annual sales from exporting	_____
in exchange for ...	_____
licensing agreements	_____
ensure quality control	_____
initial investment	_____
comparative advantages	_____
overseas sales distribution network	_____
the former Soviet states	_____

There are several methods by which firms conduct international business. The most common methods are these:
- International trade
- Licensing
- Franchising
- Joint ventures
- Acquisitions of existing operations
- Establishing new foreign subsidiaries

Each method is discussed in turn, with some emphasis on its risk and return characteristics.

International Trade

International trade is a relatively conservative approach that can be used by firms to penetrate markets (by exporting) or to obtain supplies at a low cost (by importing). There is minimal risk to this approach, since the firm does not place any of its capital at risk.[1] If the firm experiences a decline in its exporting or importing, it can normally reduce or discontinue this part of its business at a low cost.

Many large US-based MNCs, including Boeing, DuPont, General Electric, and IBM, generate more than $4 billion in annual sales from exporting. Yet, more than 20 percent of the value of all US exports is provided by small businesses.

Licensing

Licensing obligates a firm to provide its technology (copyrights, patents, trademarks, or trade names) in exchange for fees or some other specified benefits.[2] For example, AT&T and Nynex Corp. have licensing agreements to build and operate parts of India's telephone system. Sprint Corp. has a licensing agreement to develop telecommunications services in the United Kingdom. Eli Lilly & Co. has a licensing agreement to produce drugs for Hungary and other countries. IGA Inc., which operates more than 3,000 supermarkets in the United States, has a licensing agreement to operate supermarkets in China and Singapore. Licensing allows firms to use their technology in foreign markets without a major investment in foreign countries, and without the transportation costs that result from exporting.[3] A major disadvantage of licensing is that it is difficult for the firm providing the technology to ensure quality control in the foreign production process.

Franchising

Franchising obligates a firm to provide a specialized sales or service strategy, support assistance, and possibly an initial investment in the franchise in exchange for periodic fees.[4] For example, McDonald's, Pizza Hut, Subway Sandwiches, Blockbuster Video, Micro Age Computers, and Dairy Queen have franchises that are owned and managed by local residents in many foreign countries. Like licensing, franchising allows firms to penetrate foreign markets without a major investment in foreign countries. The recent relaxation of barriers in foreign countries throughout Eastern Europe and South America has resulted in numerous franchising arrangements.[5]

Joint Ventures

A joint venture is a venture that is jointly owned and operated by two or more firms. Many firms penetrate foreign markets by engaging in a joint venture with firms that reside in those markets.[6] Most joint ventures allow two firms to apply their respective comparative advantages in a given project. For example, General Mills Inc. joined in a venture with Nestlé SA, so that the cereals produced by General Mills could be sold through the overseas sales distribution network established by Nestlé.

Xerox Corp. and Fuji Co. (of Japan) engaged in a joint venture that allowed Xerox Corp. to penetrate the Japanese market and allowed Fuji to enter the photocopying business. Sara Lee Corp. and Southwestern Bell have engaged in joint ventures with Mexican firms, as such ventures have allowed entry into Mexico's markets. There are numerous joint ventures between automobile manufacturers, as each manufacturer can offer its technological advantages. General Motors has ongoing joint ventures with automobile manufacturers in several different countries, including Hungary and the former Soviet states.

Notes

[1] There is minimal risk to this approach, since the firm does not place any of its capital at risk.

【译文】采取这一途径的风险最低,因为公司不冒任何资本风险。

【解析】at risk 意为"有危险;冒风险",place ... at risk 是"冒……风险;把……置于风险之中"的意思,place any of its capital at risk 直译为"冒资本风险"。

[2] Licensing obligates a firm to provide its technology (copyrights, patents, trademarks, or trade names) in exchange for fees or some other specified benefits.

【译文】在许可经营模式下,公司有义务提供包括版权、专利、商标或品牌名在内的技术,以换取一定的费用或其他特定的利益。

【解析】license 亦作 licence。license 作名词时,是"许可;许可证"的意思;而作动词时,则是"许可;批准"的意思,如:
This shop is licensed to sell tobacco.
这家商店获准出售烟草制品。
licensing 在商务英语中是指"许可经营"这种经营模式。
obligate 意为"使在道义上(或法律上)负有责任;使负有义务",如:
At the maturity date of a note, the maker is obligated to pay the principal plus interest.
在票据到期时,出票人有义务支付本息。
in exchange for 意为"作为(对……的)交换",如:
Revenue generally is considered to be realized when there is a receipt of cash or a claim to cash in exchange for goods or services.
当作为售出商品或服务的交换而收悉现金或对现金的要求权时,一般就认为实现了收益。

[3] Licensing allows firms to use their technology in foreign markets without a major investment in foreign countries, and without the transportation costs that result from exporting.

【译文】在许可经营模式下,公司无须在国外投入大量资金,也不必支付出口带来的运输成本就可以在外国市场使用自己的技术。

【解析】该句的翻译对语序进行了调整。英语通常开门见山,直奔主题,先说结果后说条件。汉语通常根据一定的逻辑顺序按照由条件到结果,有先有后,有主有次地逐层叙述。译文将原句中句末的两个条件状语 without ..., and without ... 提前,而将主句表达的内容后译,符合汉语先条件后结果的逻辑表达习惯。

[4] Franchising obligates a firm to provide a specialized sales or service strategy, support assistance, and possibly an initial investment in the franchise in exchange for periodic fees.

【译文】在特许经营模式下,公司有义务向加盟店提供专门的销售或服务策略、支持协助或者初期投资,而加盟店必须定期向其支付一定的费用。

【解析】franchise 是"特许代理权;加盟权"的意思,franchising 在这里指"特许经营"这种经营模式。原句句末 in the franchise 中的 franchise,从上下文中可以理解其具体是指"加盟店",这里体现了英汉两种语言对具体表达和抽象表达的不同使用习惯。另外值得注意的是,在保险行业中,franchise 的中文意思是"保险免赔限度",如:

The insurance company here covers this risk with a franchise of 5%, that is, no liability attaches to the underwriter for claims below 5%.

这里的保险公司以5%的免赔限度接受这一险种,即保险商对5%以下的损失不负责任。

[5] The recent relaxation of barriers in foreign countries throughout Eastern Europe and South America has resulted in numerous franchising arrangements.

【译文】近来,整个东欧和南美国家放松了贸易壁垒,因此导致众多特许经营协定的达成。

【解析】trade barriers 是指限制外国商品和劳务进口的种种措施,分关税壁垒(tariff barrier)和非关税壁垒(non-tariff barrier)两大类。前者指对进口商品征收高额关税;后者包括除关税以外的一切限制和阻止商品进口的措施,如进口配额、外汇管制、苛刻的卫生标准等。

[6] Many firms penetrate foreign markets by engaging in a joint venture with firms that reside in those markets.

【译文】许多公司通过与当地公司合资的方式渗透到外国市场。

【解析】engage in 意为"从事;参加",如:

We are engaged in both import and export business.

我们从事进出口业务。

joint venture 指"合资"或"合资公司"。

firms that reside in those markets 是指"当地公司"。

Passage B (English-Chinese Translation)

International Business Methods (II)
Jeff Madura

Words & Expressions

Work on the following words and expressions and write the translated version in the space provided:

have full control over ...	_____
a large portion of foreign market share	_____
foreign operations	_____
partial international acquisitions	_____
expose ... to less risk	_____
a customer base	_____
extend from ...	_____
direct foreign investment	_____
the optimal method	_____
derive from ...	_____

Acquisitions of Existing Operations

Firms frequently acquire other firms in foreign countries as a means of penetrating foreign markets.[1] For example, American Express recently acquired offices in London, while Procter & Gamble recently purchased a bleach company in Panama. Acquisitions allow firms to have full control over their foreign businesses and to quickly obtain a large portion of foreign market share. However, an acquisition of existing corporations is normally riskier than the other methods previously mentioned because of the large investment required. In addition, if the foreign operations perform poorly, it may be difficult to sell the operations at a reasonable price.

Some firms engage in partial international acquisitions in order to obtain a stake in foreign operations. This requires a smaller investment than full international acquisitions and therefore exposes the firm to less risk. On the other hand, the firm will not have complete control over foreign operations that are partially acquired.

Establishing New Foreign Subsidiaries

Firms can also penetrate foreign markets by establishing new operations in foreign countries to produce and sell their products. Like a foreign acquisition, this method requires a large investment. The establishment of new subsidiaries may be preferred to foreign acquisitions because the operations can be tailored exactly to the firm's needs.[2] In addition, the investment amount may be less than that required to purchase existing operations. However, the firm will not reap any rewards from the investment until the subsidiary is built and a customer base established.[3]

Summary of Methods

The methods of increasing international business extend from the relatively simple approach of international trade to the more complex approach of acquiring foreign firms or establishing new subsidiaries.[4] Any method of increasing international business that requires a direct investment in foreign operations normally is referred to as a direct foreign investment (DFI). International trade and licensing usually are not considered to be DFI because they do not involve direct investment in foreign operations. Franchising and joint ventures tend to require some investment in foreign operations, but to a limited degree. Foreign acquisitions and the establishment of new foreign subsidiaries require substantial investment in foreign operations and represent the largest portion of DFI.[5]

The optimal method for increasing international business may depend on the characteristics of the MNC. Some MNCs, such as Exxon and the Coca-Cola Company, derive most of their revenue from outside the United States. Yet, the Coca-Cola Company engages in various licensing agreements to derive some of its foreign revenue, so it does not require as much direct foreign investment to generate its foreign revenue.[6]

Notes

[1] Firms frequently acquire other firms in foreign countries as a means of penetrating foreign markets.

【译文】公司经常以收购其他外国公司作为渗透外国市场的手段。

【解析】acquire 在商务英语中是"并购;收购;购置"的意思,如:

Some individuals prefer to acquire shares of firms that pay few dividends but have high growth potential accompanied by rapidly rising stock prices.

有些人喜欢购买那种股息分配虽然不多,但是发展潜力大、股价升值快的公司的股票。

名词 acquisition 意为"收购/并购(企业)"。

[2] The establishment of new subsidiaries may be preferred to foreign acquisitions because the operations can be tailored exactly to the firm's needs.

【译文】比起对外收购,建立新的子公司更受欢迎,因为子公司可以严格按照公司的需求经营。

【解析】subsidiary 是"子公司,附属公司"的意思; tailor to ... 意思是"使适合……的需要",如:

The accounting profession has managed to tailor its reports to satisfy these users, resulting in a variety of presentations and disclosures.

会计业已使自己的报告适合于这些用户的需要,结果就有了各种各样的报告和会计事项的公告。

[3] However, the firm will not reap any rewards from the investment until the subsidiary is built and a customer base established.

【译文】但是,在子公司建立并形成一定的客户基础以前,公司不会从投资中获得任何回报。

【解析】customer base 是指公司赖以生存的客户基础。

这个句子汉译时对语序进行了调整,将原句中后置的条件状语提前,以使译文更加符合汉语表达习惯。

[4] The methods of increasing international business extend from the relatively simple approach of international trade to the more complex approach of acquiring foreign firms or establishing new subsidiaries.

【译文】从开展国际贸易到收购外国公司或建立新的子公司,拓展国际商务的途径由相对简单逐渐走向复杂。

【解析】英语重主语、重结构,而汉语重主题、重内容。虽然原句主谓清晰,结构简单,意思理解起来也比较容易,但是句子较长,译成汉语时不可能像原句一样不用断句就可以表达清楚,所以参考译文抓住原文主题,即"拓展国际商务的途径由相对简单到逐渐复杂",把"开展国际贸易"这一简单途径和"收购外国公司或建立新的子公司"这一复杂途径放到句首,译成"从……到……"结构,与后面主题句的结构基本一致,做到形式上工整,内容上也切合原意。

[5] Foreign acquisitions and the establishment of new foreign subsidiaries require substantial investment in foreign operations and represent the largest portion of DFI.

【译文】收购外国公司和建立新的国外子公司需要对外投入大笔资金,因而占据了对外直接投资的主要份额。

【解析】represent the largest portion of DFI 在这里译作"占据了对外直接投资的主要份额",也可译为"是对外直接投资的重要组成部分"。

[6] Yet, the Coca-Cola Company engages in various licensing agreements to derive some of its foreign revenue, so it does not require as much direct foreign investment to generate its foreign revenue.

【译文】然而,可口可乐公司的许多国外收入来源于其签订的各种许可经营协定,所以不需要进行大量对外直接投资来获得国外收入。

【解析】licensing agreements 在此译作"许可经营协定",以便与前文(Passage A)中出现的"许可经营模式下"的用法相一致。licensing agreements 本义是指"许可(证)贸易协定"。协定的主要条款包括许可证费用、技术转让限制、技术诀窍的保密、技术的有效保证、协定期满后技术继续使用权等。

Passage C (Chinese-English Translation)

中国特许经营信息滞后给"假洋品牌"可乘之机

自零售业市场开放以来,特许经营已成为跨国企业在中国市场发展的重要方式之一。中国连锁经营协会行业信息部发布的中国特许经营国际企业调查中指出:目前国内许多行业的特许品牌纷纷打出意大利、荷兰、法国的优秀连锁品牌的牌子,但事实上,有近半数是子虚乌有的;当这些"假洋品牌"做出欺诈行为后,更是让加盟者蒙受了很大的经济损失。相对于西方的发达经济,中国的经济环境是比较封闭的,很多信息上的滞后和不对称直接让"假洋品牌"有可乘之机。除受假洋品牌侵蚀外,已经进入中国的真洋品牌因特许经营费用等要求过于苛刻也出现了部分水土不服的现象。部分原因是中外双方对于特许经营费用的理解和征收有异议。加盟海外特许品牌,尤其是成功的知名品牌,都要缴纳相关的特许经营费,以获得商标使用权、KNOW-HOW 等。但国内许多开展特许经营的企业,为了获得数量上的快速增长,跑马圈地,往往不收取任何特许经营费用,这样就必然导致投资洋品牌的人在心理上承受较大的不悦。

Translation Exercises

1. The proprietor is legally obligated to assume all debts of the business as personal debts.
2. A franchise is a contract between two parties granting the franchisee certain rights and privileges.
3. An acquisition is a combination in which one company acquires control of another company but both companies continues to exist as legal entities.
4. When a corporation expands its activities across its borders and engages in international trade, it could be on the way to becoming a multinational corporation.
5. 公司的整个前途受到威胁。(at risk)
6. 我们相信这些订货不久可得到批准。(license)
7. 卖方把商品让与买方,以此交换现金或日后付款的承诺。(in exchange for)
8. 我们能够使我们的保险业务适合你们的特殊需要。(tailor to)

Passage A (English-Chinese Translation)

Why Firms Become Multinational Enterprises

Words & Expressions

Work on the following words and expressions and write the translated version in the space provided:

set up operations _____
diminish the negative effects of economic swings _____
tap the growing world market _____
in response to ... _____
increased foreign competition _____
"internationalization" of control within the MNE _____
tariff walls _____
take advantage of technological expertise _____
provide access to ... _____
reclaim one's exclusive rights _____
protect one's international competitiveness _____

Companies become MNEs for a number of reasons. One is to protect themselves from the risks and uncertainties of the domestic business cycle.[1] By setting up operations in another country, they can often diminish the negative effects of economic swings in the home country. This is a form of international diversification.

A second reason is to tap the growing world market for goods and services. This is part of the process of globalization, the rapid growth of similar goods and services produced and distributed by MNEs on a world scale. For example, many foreign MNEs have targeted the United States because of its large population and high per capita income. It is the world's single largest market in terms of gross national product. Americans have both a desire for new goods and services and the money to buy them. For the same reason, US MNEs have been targeting Europe and Asia as primary areas for the twenty-first century. [2]

Firms also become MNEs in response to increased foreign competition and to protect world market shares. Using a "follow the competitor" strategy, an MNE will set up operations in the home countries of competitors. This approach serves a dual purpose: (1) it takes away business from competitors, and (2) it lets others know that if they attack the MNE's home market, they will face a similar response. This strategy of staking out global market shares is particularly important when MNEs want to communicate the conditions under which they will retaliate. [3]

A fourth reason to become an MNE is the desire to reduce costs. By setting up operations close to the foreign customer, MNEs can eliminate transportation costs, avoid the expenses associated with having middlemen handle the product, respond more accurately and rapidly to customer needs, and take advantage of local resources. This process, known as "internationalization" of control within the MNE, can help to reduce overall costs.

A fifth reason is to overcome tariff walls by serving a foreign market from within. The EU provides an excellent example. Firms outside the EU are subject to tariffs on goods exported to EU countries. [4] Firms producing the goods within the EU can transport them to any other country in the bloc without paying tariffs. The same is now occurring in North America, thanks to the North American Free Trade Agreement (NAFTA), which eliminates tariffs between Canada, the United States, and Mexico.

A sixth reason for becoming an MNE is to take advantage of technological expertise by manufacturing goods directly rather than allowing others to do it under a license. A license agreement is a contractual arrangement in which one firm, the licensor, provides access to some of its patents, trademarks, or technology to another firm, the licensee, in exchange for a fee or royalty. [5] This fee often involves a fixed amount upon signing the contract and then a royalty of 2 to 5 percent on sales generated by the arrangement. A typical licensing contract will run five to seven years and be renewable at the option of either or both parties. [6] Although the benefits of a licensing agreement are obvious, in recent years some MNEs have concluded that it is unwise to give another firm access to proprietary information such as patents, trademarks, or technological expertise, and they have allowed these arrangements to lapse. This allows them to reclaim their exclusive rights and then to manufacture and directly sell the products in overseas markets. This direct involvement in foreign markets brings the company closer to emerging technological developments, helping to prepare it to respond by acquiring the new technology or by developing substitutes. As a result, MNEs are better able to protect their international competitiveness than companies that have license agreements.

Notes

[1]   One is to protect themselves from the risks and uncertainties of the domestic

business cycle.

【译文】其中一个原因是为了保护自己免受国内商业周期所带来的风险以及不稳定性的冲击。

【解析】这句话的核心词组是 protect ... from ...，意为"保护……免受……"。

[2] For the same reason, US MNEs have been targeting Europe and Asia as primary areas for the twenty-first century.

【译文】出于相同的原因，美国的跨国公司一直将目标锁定在欧洲和亚洲，把这两个地区作为它们 21 世纪的主要市场。

【解析】have been doing sth. 是现在完成进行时，译为"一直……"；target 在原句中是动词，可译作"将目标定在……"；area 本义是"区域，地区"，这里根据对上下文的理解译作"市场"更为贴切。

[3] This strategy of staking out global market shares is particularly important when MNEs want to communicate the conditions under which they will retaliate.

【译文】当跨国公司想要（对外）传达在何种情况下它们会采取反击时，声明其对全球市场份额的所有权这一战略是尤其重要的。

【解析】stake out 的意思是"用桩标出地界（尤指旧时用以表明所有权），声称对（研究领域、地方等）有特殊关联或所有权"，在句中取后面一种意思。此外，原句中放在句末的时间状语从句在翻译成汉语时前置，这样比较符合汉语的表达习惯。

[4] Firms outside the EU are subject to tariffs on goods exported to EU countries.

【译文】欧盟国家以外的公司在出口商品到欧盟国家时需要承担关税。

【解析】EU = European Union，即欧洲联盟（简称欧盟），是由欧洲经济共同体（简称欧共体）（European Economic Community）发展而来的，是一个集政治实体和经济实体于一身、在世界上具有重要影响的区域一体化组织。

be subject to 意为"易受……的；以……为准的；以……为条件的"，如：

The buyers agree to buy and the sellers agree to sell the undermentioned commodity subject to terms and conditions as stipulated below.

买卖双方同意按照以下条款买卖下述商品。

[5] A license agreement is a contractual arrangement in which one firm, the licensor, provides access to some of its patents, trademarks, or technology to another firm, the licensee, in exchange for a fee or royalty.

【译文】许可协议是一种合同约定，在协议中，一家公司（许可方）将自己的专利、商标或者技术授予另一家公司（被许可方）使用，作为交换，被许可方向许可方支付一定的费用或专利使用费。

【解析】licensor 意为"许可方"，licensee 意为"被许可方"。royalty 在商务英语中有"特许开采权；专利使用费"等意思。

[6] A typical licensing contract will run five to seven years and be renewable at the option of either or both parties.

【译文】典型的许可合同的有效期是 5—7 年，在其中一方或者双方的要求下可以续签。

【解析】句中的 run 在翻译中并没有硬译为动词，而是译为"有效期"，准确地表达了意思。renewable 意为"可更新的；可展期的"，此处译为"可续签的"。

Passage B (English-Chinese Translation)

Figuring Out How to Do Business in Japan

Words & Expressions

Work on the following words and expressions and write the translated version in the space provided:

carve out a market in a country	_____
keiretsus and other cartel-like arrangement	_____
huge, vertically integrated companies	_____
ensure the survival of these stores	_____
retail margin	_____
manufacturing rebates	_____
advertising subsidies	_____
break into the Japanese market	_____
bid for business	_____
push out their major competitors	_____
get off the ground	_____
enter into a joint venture with ...	_____
share the risk and achieve rapid market access	_____
acquisition and merger	_____
a ship container leasing business	_____

Doing business in Japan presents many challenges to foreign MNEs. One of the biggest is how to carve out a market in a country where keiretsus and other cartel-like arrangements are so common. At first, many MNEs entering Japan find it difficult to compete effectively. Major keiretsus or cartels are billion-dollar firms with business ties that turn them into huge, vertically integrated companies.[1] Some of these cartels own or have business dealings with a host of other companies that ensure that the keiretsu can manufacture and sell its products without ever relying on a firm outside this circle of firms. There are even distribution cartels in Japan that are so encompassing that they can control the flow of products, accessories, services, and prices from the factory floor all the way to the consumer.[2] A good example is Matsushita.

Matsushita manufactures Panasonic, National, Technics, and Quasar products. The firm also controls a chain of approximately 25,000 national retail stores throughout the country, which collectively generate more than 50 percent of the company's domestic sales. These stores sell a wide variety of products, from batteries to refrigerators. Most importantly, they agree to sell at manufacturers' recommended prices. In turn Matsushita ensures the survival of these stores by giving them a 25 percent retail margin on sales. This margin is a result of fixed retail prices, manufacturing rebates, advertising subsidies, and protected sales territories from other Matsushita dealers.[3] Other Japanese firms have similar arrangements. Examples include Toshiba, Hitachi, Mitsubishi, Sanyo, and Sony, which, along with Matsushita, collectively control approximately 70,000 small retail stores (about 7.5 percent of those in the entire country).

Despite such a major obstacle, foreign MNEs are learning that there are a number of useful strategies that can help them to break into the Japanese market. In the case of suppliers, for example, it is important to be patient and to continue to bid for business. At first, many keiretsus turn down foreign companies because they want to stay within their cartel-like arrangement. However, these keiretsus are also interested in pushing out their major competitors, and a foreign supplier with high-quality products will often find that one of the major keiretsus will break with tradition and make a deal.[4] Additionally, many small keiretsus are trying to get off the ground and to gain market shares. These too are interested in developing relations with high-quality suppliers. Moreover, because the best local suppliers are usually already tied to keiretsus, foreign sources are often very attractive to these fledgling cartels.

A second strategy is to link forces with established Japanese firms in the form of joint ventures.[5] For example, T. Row Price Associates recently entered into a joint venture with Daiwa Securities and the Sumitomo Bank. The venture will focus on mutual-fund management. And the Swiss Bank Corporation has now formed a host of new joint ventures with the Long-Term Credit Bank of Japan Limited. While there are drawbacks to these ventures, two of the major advantages are sharing the risk and achieving rapid market access.

A third strategy is to team up with Japanese firms to help develop or manufacture new products. One recent example is Motorola and Texas Instruments (TI), which have an arrangement with Sony. TI provides signal processors for Sony compact disc players and Motorola manufactures the chips that go into Sony camcorders. Another example is AT&T's Bell Laboratories and AT&T's Microelectronics, which have a working relationship with NEC. Bell is helping NEC to design products and Microelectronics is making and supplying the chips for these units.

A fourth, and more recent, strategy is acquisition and merger. GE Capital, for example, has bought the leasing businesses of the Japan Leasing Corporation, purchased NC Card Sendai, specialists in financing for installment sales and consumer credit, and set up a merger with a Japanese firm to expand a ship container leasing business.

There are a number of reasons that MNEs want to do business in Japan. One is the growing market. A second is that Japan is a major economic force in the Pacific and this power is likely to grow over the ensuing decades. By maintaining a presence in Japan worldwide competitors are in the best position to monitor these strategies and to respond with countermeasures. [6] For these multinationals, doing business in Japan is critical to the growth of their enterprises. So it is critical for them to learn how to do business here.

Notes

[1] Major keiretsus or cartels are billion-dollar firms with business ties that turn them into huge, vertically integrated companies.

【译文】主要的日本经联组织或企业联合中的公司都是身价数十亿美金的公司,它们的商业纽带使得他们成为庞大的纵向联合公司。

【解析】keiretsus(a Japanese term meaning a network of linked corporations)表示"日本经联组织"。日本经联组织是垂直整合许多厂商,彼此间密切联系及合作的大型组织。通常经联组织并不是以权力关系为联结,而是以跨公司的所有权、长期协定、联合董事会或是社会关系联结(如许多家公司的高阶主管曾经是同学)等。cartel 意为"企业联合",也称"卡特尔"(音译)。

[2] There are even distribution cartels in Japan that are so encompassing that they can control the flow of products, accessories, services, and prices from the factory floor all the way to the consumer.

【译文】在日本甚至还有分销企业联合,它们的涵盖面很广,以至于它们可以自工厂到客户一路控制产品、零配件、服务以及价格的流动。

【解析】encompass 意为"包含,包括;环绕",因此这里把 encompassing 理解为"涵盖面很广"。

[3] This margin is a result of fixed retail prices, manufacturing rebates, advertising subsidies, and protected sales territories from other Matsushita dealers.

【译文】这笔利润来自固定的零售价格、生产折扣、广告补贴以及公司保护下的销售领域,这些领域不受其他松下产品经销商的影响。

【解析】margin 指的是"成本与售价之间的差额、赢利及利润";rebate 指"(债、税)等的可减免的款额、折扣或部分退款",句中应理解为"生产过程中的折扣"。
Matsushita 即"松下电气工业公司",它是电器业巨人,位于大阪,以 Panasonic, National, Technics 和 Quasar 品牌制造电子产品。

[4] However, these keiretsus are also interested in pushing out their major competitors, and a foreign supplier with high-quality products will often find that one of the major keiretsus will break with tradition and make a deal.

【译文】然而,这些日本经联组织成员也有兴致排挤它们的主要竞争对手,因此,一家拥有高质量产品的外国供应商经常会发现一个日本经联组织的主要成员会打破传统,与其达成交易。

【解析】be interested in 意为"对……感兴趣",但是这里如果这样译,不符合句子的总体风格,所以将其译为"有兴致……";push out 原意为"把……推出去",此处根据语境译为"排挤"更加合适。

［5］ A second strategy is to link forces with established Japanese firms in the form of joint ventures.

【译文】第二个战略就是以合资企业的形式与已建立完善的日本公司强强联手。

【解析】joint venture 表示"合资企业"。我们通常所说的三资企业包括：合资企业（joint venture）、合作企业（cooperative enterprise）和外商独资企业（exclusively foreign-funded corporation）。

［6］ By maintaining a presence in Japan worldwide competitors are in the best position to monitor these strategies and to respond with countermeasures.

【译文】通过维持在日本的一席之地，全球的竞争者能够最有效地掌握这些战略，并以相应的对策作出回应。

【解析】in the best position 可作"居于最好的位置"讲，但此意放入句中不妥，故意译为"能够最有效地"；而 in position 意为"在适当的位置；就位，到位"。
counter-是否定前缀，表示方向或作用相反，countermeasure 译为"对策"；因此，counter-attack 可译为"反攻，反击"，counteract 则可译为"对抗；抵消"等。

Passage C (Chinese-English Translation)

大力实施本土化战略

实施本土化对跨国公司来讲是一项十分重要，并且是一箭双雕的战略决策。它不但能有效降低向东道国派遣高级管理人员的成本，与此同时，还能充分利用东道国相对低廉的人力资源。从长远来看，把当地优秀的经理人员提拔到决策者的位子上来是十分明智的选择，因为他们比较熟悉本国的法律法规，了解本国的市场行情，绝无文化方面的障碍，并能有效地与当地各部门进行沟通。简而言之，他们更熟悉本国政府制定的游戏规则。但要吸引并留住这些优秀人才，跨国公司必须做一件实实在在的事情：即给他们提供自身发展和事业进步的机遇。以中国这个新兴市场国家为例，跨国公司对其投资与日俱增，如今它吸引的外商投资总量仅次于当今的头号发达国家——美国，因而跨国公司对中国本土优秀人才的竞争便十分激烈。他们明白一个简单的道理：市场竞争归根结底是人才的竞争，谁掌握了人才谁就占尽了先机，再配以雄厚的资本、先进的技术以及行之有效的管理方法和运作手段，他们也就掌握了搏击市场风浪、克敌制胜的法宝。比如苏州迅达电梯有限公司和欧莱雅公司，通过实施本土化战略，均取得了斐然的业绩。

Translation Skills（Ⅰ）

定语从句的翻译

英语和汉语属于不同的语系和不同的语言形态，体现在句子结构上的显著特征是汉语重意合，英语重形合。所谓形合，就是句子的语法意义和逻辑意义是通过词语与分句之间用自身的形式手段（如关联词）体现。因此，英语句子常用各种形式手段，如连接词语、分句或从句,注重显性衔接,句子形式完整,结构紧凑严谨,注重以形显义。而意合是指词语和分句之间不用语言形式手段连接,句子中的语法意义和逻辑意义是通过词语和分句的含义来表达。因此汉语句子注重逻辑事理顺序和句子的功能、意义,通过隐性连贯以神通形,结构简练明快。英语句子和汉语句子的差别要求我们在英汉翻译的过程中要进行句子结构的转化。在本章,我们就商务英语翻译中定语从句的翻译作详细讲解。

针对定语从句的翻译,我们总结出以下几种常用方法:

1. 定语前置法

前置法也就是将定语从句翻译成带"的"的定语词组,放在先行词之前,从而将复合句翻译成汉语单句。但是这种翻译方法的局限性比较大,它只适用于定语从句部分不太长的限制性定语从句。

例1 Most customers accept credit cards which are safe, fast and convenient.

译文:多数顾客接受了安全、快捷且方便的信用卡。

2. 定语后置法

后置法使用的范围相对比较广泛,它适用于从句部分比较长而且复杂的限制性定语从句和起补充说明的非限制性定语从句。这种译法就是将从句译成和主句并列的一个分句,放在主句之后,可以用句号隔开主句,并且重复先行词。

例2 Ours is a profession which traditionally has been guided by a precept that transcends the virtue of uttering the truth for truth's sake.

译文:我们这个职业传统上恪守这样一个信条,这个信条胜过为讲真话而讲真话的美德。

3. 融合法

融合法,顾名思义,就是将主句与从句融合在一起,利用从句的关系代词与主句某成分的代替关系,根据意思重新组成汉语单句。英语中there be 结构的汉译通常采用这种译法。

例3 There are many competing technologies that can be used to perform database interaction, shopping cart functions, and interactive/dynamic content presentation.

译文:许多有竞争力的技术可以用来实现数据库交互、购物车功能、交互/动态内容陈列。

4. 转换为状语从句

其实,在很多的定语从句中,从句和主句之间还存在着状语关系,因而译者可以根据原句的逻辑关系,将原句译成汉语中表明因果关系、转折关系、条件关系、让步关系的偏正复句。因此,在翻译中要善于从英语原句的字里行间发现这些逻辑上的关系。此种译法在限制性定语从句和非限制性定语从句中均适用。

例4 In office, figures, lists and information are compiled which tell the managers or heads of the business what is happening in their shops or factories.

译文:在办公室里,工作人员将各种数据、表格和信息加以汇编,以便让经理或主管人员了解他们的商店或工厂目前正在发生的情况。

在上文中,我们讲了定语从句的各种翻译方法,在这里我们还要提醒大家,在翻译含有定语从句的句子时,我们应该特别注意在分析句子的结构上面下功夫,务必要搞清定语从句所修饰的先行词是哪一个。确定定语从句的先行词是极为重要的,做出正确的判断的关键在于分析句子的结构和句子所出现的上下文。另外,我们还要注意一些比较复杂的定语从句结构,也就是那些定语从句里又含有定语从句的情况,在翻译这类句子时我们应该注意灵活运用我们在前面讲述的一些翻译技巧,尤其要注意分析各个定语从句之间的关系,可以对原句进行合理地拆译。

例5 Behaviourists suggest that the child **who** is raised in an environment **where** there are many stimuli which develop his or her capacity for appropriate responses will experience greater intellectual development.

译文:行为主义者认为,如果一个儿童在有许多刺激物的环境中成长,而这些刺激物能够发展其作出适当反应的能力,那么这个儿童将会有更高的智力发展。

在商务英语中,定语从句是相当普遍的,要想理解原句的意思,分析原句的结构是相当重要的。以上翻译方法、翻译技巧以及翻译中的注意点在商务英语的翻译中定会起到不容忽视的作用。

Translation Exercises

1. This Agreement is renewable for a further period upon mutual consent after consultation among all parties concerned.
2. One of the characteristics of a multinational enterprise is that affiliated firms are linked by ties of common ownership.
3. MNEs make decisions based primarily on what is best for the company, even if this means transferring funds or jobs to other countries.
4. The orchestra were all in position, waiting for the conductor.
5. 建立工会是为了保护矿工的权利和利益不受侵犯。(protect ... from ...)
6. 他把盈利的10%划归自己所有。(stake out)
7. 我们须遵守当地的法律。(be subject to)
8. 这是为防止一触即发的罢工而采取的对策。(countermeasure)

Unit 3

Passage A (English-Chinese Translation)

Six Rules of Thumb for Doing Business across Cultures

Words & Expressions

Work on the following words and expressions and write the translated version in the space provided:

rules of thumb	_____
social and business etiquette	_____
American-style crisp business relationships	_____
personal relationship and trust	_____
talent with idiom and imagery	_____
surface culture	_____
deep culture	_____
cultural differences	_____
strategic advantage	_____
the departure of competent employees	_____

  Knowing your customer is just as important anywhere in the world as it is at home, whether one is aiming to sell computers in Abidjan or soft drinks in Kuala Lumpur. Each culture has its logic, and within that logic are real, sensible reasons for the way foreigners do things.[1] If the salesperson can figure out the basic pattern of the culture, he or she will be more effective interacting with foreign clients and colleagues. The following six rules of thumb are helpful.

  (1) Be prepared. Whether traveling abroad or selling from home, no one should approach a foreign market without doing his or her homework. A mentor is most desirable, complemented by endless reading on social and business etiquette, history and folklore, current affairs (including current relations between your two countries), the culture's values, geography, sources of pride (artists, musicians, sports), religion, political structure, and practical matters such as currency and hours of business. Mimi Murphy, an exporter who trades primarily in Indonesia, says, "Whenever I travel, the first

thing I do in any town is read the newspaper. Then when I meet my customer, I can talk about the sports or the news of the day. He knows that I am interested in the things he is interested in, and he will want to do business with me."

(2) Slow down. Americans are clock-watchers. Time is money. In many countries, Americans are seen to be in a rush, in other words, unfriendly, arrogant, and untrustworthy. Almost everywhere, we must learn to wait patiently.

(3) Establish trust. Often American-style crisp business relationships will get the sales representative nowhere.[2] Product quality, pricing, and clear contracts are not as important as the personal relationship and trust that are developed carefully and sincerely over time. The market must be established as simpatico, worthy of the business, and dependable in the long run.

(4) Understand the importance of language. Obviously, copy must be translated by a professional who speaks both languages fluently, with a vocabulary sensitive to nuance and connotation, as well as talent with idiom and imagery in each culture.[3] An interpreter is often critical and may be helpful even when one of the parties speaks the other's language.

(5) Respect the culture. Manners are important. The traveling sales representative is a guest in the country and must respect the hosts' rules. As a Saudi Arabian official states in one of the *Going International* films, Americans in foreign countries have a tendency to treat the natives as foreigners, and they forget that actually it is they who are the foreigners themselves.

(6) Understand components of culture. A region is a sort of cultural iceberg with two components: surface culture (fads, style, food, etc.) and deep culture (attitudes, beliefs, values).[4] Less than 15 percent of a region's culture is visible, and strangers to the culture must look below the surface. Consider the British habit of automatically lining up on the sidewalk when waiting for a bus. This surface cultural trait results from the deep cultural desire to lead neat and controlled lives.[5]

Knowledge about other cultures and how they affect the way people do business may show businesspeople working in a culture different from their own that their solutions are not always the appropriate ones for a given task. Understanding this is the first step in learning to use cultural differences to gain a strategic advantage.

Mishandling or ignoring cultural differences can cause numerous problems, such as lost sales, the departure of competent employees, and low morale that contributes to low productivity. However, when these differences are blended successfully, they can result in innovative business practices superior to those that either culture could produce by itself.[6]

Notes

[1]　Each culture has its logic, and within that logic are real, sensible reasons for the way foreigners do things.

【译文】每一种文化都有自身的逻辑,这种逻辑中存在着外国人处事方式的真实合理的原因。

【解析】原句本身就是两个分句,所以采用直译方法比较自然合理;如果合二为一的话句子将是"每一种文化都有解释外国人处事方式的真实合理的原因的逻辑",这样的翻译未尝不可,只是定语部分过于冗长复杂。

[2] Often American-style crisp business relationships will get the sales representative nowhere.

【译文】干脆利落的美国式商业关系将会使销售代理劳而无功。

【解析】crisp 本义是"脆的,易碎的",在本句中可以理解为美国人办事的"干脆利落";sales representative 是"销售代理"的意思。

get ... nowhere 意为"(使)无进展,(使)徒劳",如:

Unreasonable treatment of the workers will get the firm nowhere.

对职工的不合理待遇会使这家商行得不偿失。

[3] Obviously, copy must be translated by a professional who speaks both languages fluently, with a vocabulary sensitive to nuance and connotation, as well as talent with idiom and imagery in each culture.

【译文】很明显,从事文字翻译工作的应该是一名专业人员,他能流利地讲两种语言,他的词汇量使他对语言的细微差别和言外之意很敏感,他还对每一种文化中的习语和比喻很有天赋。

【解析】这句话定语部分是比较长的定语从句,选择后置法翻译比较合适,也就是将定语作为单句逐一译出。

[4] A region is a sort of cultural iceberg with two components: surface culture (fads, style, food, etc.) and deep culture (attitudes, beliefs, values).

【译文】一个地区就是一种文化冰山,其中有两种成分:表层文化(如时尚、风格、食品等)和深层文化(如观点、信仰、价值观等)。

【解析】surface culture 和 deep culture 分别译为"表层文化"和"深层文化",这是两个相互对应又互为补充的概念。

[5] This surface cultural trait results from the deep cultural desire to lead neat and controlled lives.

【译文】这种表层文化的特点产生于深层文化的渴望,即对想要过一种井然有序的生活的渴望。

【解析】result from 意思是"由于……发生,从……产生"。

[6] However, when these differences are blended successfully, they can result in innovative business practices superior to those that either culture could produce by itself.

【译文】然而,当这些不同之处成功融合的时候,它们可以产生出新颖的商业手段,这些手段比任何一种文化自身创造出来的都要优越。

【解析】result in 意思是"产生某种作用或结果"。本句的翻译只要注意句末 practices 的定语处理即可,这里把这个定语译成了一个单句,结构清晰,意思明了。practice 根据上下文理解为"商业手段"。

Passage B (English-Chinese Translation)

Managing Corporate Culture

Words & Expressions

Work on the following words and expressions and write the translated version in the space provided:

exert influence on ...	_____
a strong culture	_____
rest on ...	_____
preserve stable relationships	_____
patterns of behavior	_____
an optimal culture	_____
manage corporate culture	_____
strategy-culture compatibility	_____
minor structural modifications	_____
top management	_____
have a strategic vision	_____
monetary rewards	_____

Because an organization's culture can exert a powerful influence on the behavior of all employees, it can strongly affect a company's ability to shift its strategic direction. A problem for a strong culture is that a change in mission, objectives, strategies, or policies is not likely to be successful if it is in opposition to the accepted culture of the company. Corporate culture has a strong tendency to resist change because its very reason for existence often rests on preserving stable relationships and patterns of behavior.[1] For example, the male-dominated, Japanese-centered corporate culture of the giant Mitsubishi Corporation created problems for the company when it implemented its growth strategy in North America. The alleged sexual harassment of its female employees by male supervisors resulted in a lawsuit by the US Equal Employment Opportunity Commission and a boycott of the company's automobiles by the National Organization for Women.

There is no best corporate culture. An optimal culture is one that best supports the mission and strategy of the company of which it is a part. This means that, like structure and staffing, corporate culture should support the strategy. Unless strategy is in complete agreement with the culture, any significant change in strategy should be followed by a modification of the organization's culture.[2] Although corporate culture can be changed, it may often take a long time and it requires much effort. A key job of management involves managing corporate culture. In doing so, management must evaluate what a particular change in strategy means to the corporate culture, assess if a change in culture is needed, and decide if an attempt to change the culture is worth the likely costs.

Assessing Strategy-Culture Compatibility

When implementing a new strategy, a company should take the time to assess strategy-culture compatibility. Consider the following questions regarding the corporation's culture:

1. Is the planned strategy compatible with the company's current culture? *If yes*, full steam ahead. Tie organizational changes into the company's culture by identifying how the new strategy will achieve the mission better than the current strategy does. [3] *If not ...*

2. Can the culture be easily modified to make it more compatible with the new strategy? *If yes*, move forward carefully by introducing a set of culture-changing activities such as minor structural modifications, training and development activities, and/or hiring new managers who are more compatible with the new strategy. When Procter & Gamble's top management decided to implement a strategy aimed at reducing costs, for example, it made some changes in how things were done, but it did not eliminate its brand-management system. The culture adapted to these modifications over a couple years and productivity increased. *If not ...*

3. Is management willing and able to make major organizational changes and accept probable delays and a likely increase in costs? *If yes*, manage around the culture by establishing a new structural unit to implement the new strategy. At General Motors, for example, top management realized the company had to make some radical changes to be more competitive. [4] Because the current structure, culture, and procedures were very inflexible, management decided to establish a completely new division (GM's first new division since 1918) called Saturn to build its new auto. In cooperation with the United Auto Workers, an entirely new labor agreement was developed, based on decisions reached by consensus. Carefully selected employees received from 100 to 750 hours of training, and a whole new culture was built piece by piece. *If not ...*

4. Is management still committed to implementing the strategy? *If yes*, find a joint-venture partner or contract with another company to carry out the strategy. If not, formulate a different strategy.

Managing Cultural Change through Communication

Communication is key to the effective management of change. Rationale for strategic changes should be communicated to workers not only in newsletters and speeches, but also in training and development programs. [5] Companies in which major cultural changes have taken place successfully had the following characteristics in common:

- The CEO and other top managers had a strategic vision of what the company could become and communicated this vision to employees at all levels. The current performance of the company was compared to that of its competition and constantly updated.
- The vision was translated into the key elements necessary to accomplish that vision. [6] For example, if the vision called for the company to become a leader in quality or service, aspects of quality and service were pinpointed for improvement and appropriate measurement systems were developed to monitor them. These measures were communicated widely through contests, formal and informal recognition, and monetary rewards, among other devices.

Notes

[1] Corporate culture has a strong tendency to resist change because its very reason for existence often rests on preserving stable relationships and patterns of behavior.

【译文】公司文化有很强烈的抵制变化的趋势,因为它的存在恰好常常建立在保持稳定关系和行为模式的基础上。

【解析】reason 前面的 very 意为"正好,恰恰";rest on 是"依赖,依靠"的意思,在这里将它译成"建立在……的基础上"是根据整个句子的结构需要而定的。

[2] Unless strategy is in complete agreement with the culture, any significant change in strategy should be followed by a modification of the organization's culture.

【译文】除非战略与文化完全一致,否则战略上的任何重大变化都将带来该公司文化的变化。

【解析】be in agreement with 意为"与……一致";reach an agreement with … 意思是"与……达成协议"。

[3] Tie organizational changes into the company's culture by identifying how the new strategy will achieve the mission better than the current strategy does.

【译文】通过确认新的战略将如何比现行的战略更好地完成任务,我们可以将公司的变化与公司的文化联系起来。

【解析】这个句子本身是一个祈使句,在翻译的时候如果不加上"我们"作为主语的话,句子显得很生硬。此外,在翻译时,特意将"by …"结构提前译出,保证了句子的通顺。

[4] At General Motors, for example, top management realized the company had to make some radical changes to be more competitive.

【译文】举例来说,美国通用汽车公司的最高管理层意识到公司必须要作出根本性的变化才能更有竞争力。

【解析】General Motors 是美国通用汽车公司;top management 意为"最高管理层,上层管理人员",它是由一个机构中最高层管理人员组成的部门,这个部门通常以与董事会密切配合的总裁和副总裁为首,并包括各个处室或部门的主管,直接受其管辖的是中层管理部门(middle management)。

[5] Rationale for strategic changes should be communicated to workers not only in newsletters and speeches, but also in training and development programs.

【译文】战略变化的根本原因应当告知工人,不仅是以简讯或者演说的方式,还应该以培训或发展计划的方式。

【解析】在翻译这句话时,采用顺译法比较合适,因为如果将它翻译成"战略变化的根本原因应当不仅是以简讯或者演说的方式,还应该以培训或发展计划的方式传达给工人。"意思的表达可能是比较清晰,但整个句子读起来不流畅。

注意:注[2]的主句也是采用了顺译法,译文读来自然顺畅。

[6] The vision was translated into the key elements necessary to accomplish that vision.

【译文】这种远见被转变成实现这种远见所必需的主要元素。

【解析】这里把后置定语 necessary to accomplish that vision 前置翻译,句子比较简洁;translate 在这里译为"转化,转变成"。

Passage C (Chinese-English Translation)

尽可能使文化冲击最小化

当跨国公司的经理进入一种全新的文化中时,他很可能会经历一种"困惑",这种困惑被称之为"文化冲击"(culture shock),它使得跨国公司的经理有如迷失了方向,显得不知所措。文化冲击是一种痛苦而令人难忘的经历,它要求跨国公司的经理去应对一系列有别于自身文化的、令人眼花缭乱的新的文化信息和文化环境。它可能表现为温和的忧虑和不适,也可能是十分严重的焦躁不安或手足无措,使得跨国公司的经理无法履行其正常的职责。由于跨国公司的经理不懂当地的语言或者非言语的行为,他自己的行为也就失去了赖以评判的标准。在与东道国的同事们进行交流和沟通时,他往往会有失望、焦躁、恼怒、无奈以及因高度集中注意力所带来的紧张感。简而言之,跨国公司经理缺乏一张文化地图来帮助他预测他人的行为和期望,进而借以指导其自身的行为和期望。

文化冲击在一些外派经理们身上显得尤为突出,因为他们在相当长的一段时间里生活和工作在一种全新的文化中。事实上,外派经理失败的一种常见的解释是他们未能适应东道国的文化和社会大环境。但是,即使是在异族文化中仅待上几天的经理也会遭遇到文化冲击,这是一种对"未知数"的恼人的、挥之不去的焦虑。因此,学会接近一种全新的文化,也就是学会如何减轻文化冲击的影响。从而,为跨国公司的经理在异国他乡实现其建功立业的宏伟蓝图打下一个良好的基础。

Translation Exercises

1. A fee or percentage is allowed to a sales representative or an agent for services rendered.
2. The greater the gap between the cultures of the acquired firm and the acquiring firm, the faster executives in the acquired firm quit their jobs and valuable talent is lost.
3. He nodded in agreement with me.
4. When merging with or acquiring another company, top management must give some consideration to a potential clash of corporate cultures.
5. 扩建计划造成债务增加。(result from)
6. 经济过热可能导致通货膨胀。(result in)
7. 我们的成功取决于销售额的增加。(rest on)
8. 我们该把思想变为行动了。(translate)

Unit 4

Passage A (English-Chinese Translation)

The IMF and the World Bank Today

Words & Expressions

Work on the following words and expressions and write the translated version in the space provided:

floating exchange rates
OPEC oil price hikes
massive flows of funds
optimistic assessments
bad debts
make debt repayments
tight control over the growth of the money supply
endorse a new approach
debt reduction
debtor nation
a set of imposed conditions
macroeconomic policy management
loan projects

  Over the last couple of decades the role of the IMF has declined. Floating exchange rates have resulted in a diminished demand for short-term loans, and no major industrialized country has borrowed money from the IMF for over 20 years. Nations such as Great Britain and the United States have financed their deficits by borrowing private money rather than relying on IMF funds. [1] As a result, inspired by the OPEC oil price hikes of 1973 and 1979 and the resulting third world crisis, the IMF has found a new mission for itself.

  OPEC price increases of the 1970s resulted in massive flows of funds from major oil-importing countries such as Japan and the United States to oil producing countries that now sought investment opportunities for these monies. Commercial banks quickly stepped in to recycle these funds by borrowing from OPEC and lending to third world governments in Latin America and Africa. [2] These loans were based on optimistic assessments that proved to be highly inaccurate. A number of reasons accounted for the failure of these third world countries to generate strong economic growth including: (a) rising short-term interest rates worldwide which increased the cost of these debts; (b) poor management of the economies; (c) and a slowdown in the growth rate of the industrialized nations, the main markets for third world products.

As a result, there was a massive debt crisis. Commercial banks held over $1 trillion of bad debts and there was no hope of ever being repaid. Even Mexico, long thought to be highly creditworthy, announced that it could no longer service its $80 billion in international debt without an immediate new loan of $3 billion. [3] Brazil and Argentina, among others, also were unable to make their debt repayments. The international monetary system was on the verge of a major crisis.

This is when the IMF stepped in. Working with several Western governments including the Unite States, Mexico's debt was rescheduled, new loans were made, and an IMF-dictated series of macroeconomic policies were accepted by the Mexican government including tight control over the growth of the money supply and major cuts in government spending. [4] The IMF followed a similar approach in helping other countries. However, there was a problem with the IMF solution. It rested on the economy of these countries turning around and generating sufficient growth to repay the rescheduled debt. By the mid-1980s it was apparent that this was not happening and by 1989 it was evident that the mere rescheduling of debt was not a long-run solution to the problem. In April of that year the IMF endorsed a new approach first proposed by Nicholas Brady, US Secretary of the Treasury. [5]

The Brady Plan rested on the belief that debt reduction was a necessary part of the solution and the IMF and World Bank would have to assume roles in financing it. In essence, the plan called for the IMF, the World Bank, and the Japanese government to each contribute $10 billion to the task of debt reduction. In order to obtain these funds, each debtor nation would have to submit to a set of imposed conditions for macroeconomic policy management and debt repayment. The first application of the plan was the Mexican debt reduction of 1989 which cut that country's debt of $107 billion by about $15 billion. [6]

One result of the IMF's involvement in resolving the third world debt crisis has been the blurring of the line between itself and the World Bank. Under the original Bretton Woods agreement, the IMF was to provide short-term loans and the World Bank was to provide long-term loans.

At the same time the World Bank has been moving closer to the IMF. During the

1970s the bank found that many of its loan projects for irrigation, energy, transportation, etc. were not producing the kind of long-term economic gains that had been predicted. On close examination, the bank found that many of these projects were being undermined by the broad policy environment of the particular country. It was obvious that loan conditions needed to extend beyond the project to the economy at large.[7] So the World Bank devised a new type of loan. In addition to providing funds to support specific projects, the bank now provides loans for the government to use as it sees fit in return for promises on macroeconomic policy.[8] This, of course, is the same thing that the IMF has done in recent years, lending money to debtor nations in return for promises regarding macroeconomic policy.

Today both the IMF and the World Bank are actively involved in their new commitments in Eastern Europe. However, given that both seem to be doing similar jobs, it is quite possible that the two will eventually be merged.

Notes

[1] Nations such as Great Britain and the United States have financed their deficits by borrowing private money rather than relying on IMF funds.

【译文】像英美这样的国家都不再依赖国际货币基金组织,而是通过借入民间款项以填补赤字。

【解析】finance 这里作动词,是"(为……)筹措资金,融资"的意思,如:

Businesses constantly need funds to finance their diverse activities.

企业需要为各种经营活动不断筹措资金。

这里 finance their deficits 如果直译成"为赤字融资",会显得生硬拗口,所以翻译成"填补赤字"合乎汉语表达习惯。

[2] Commercial banks quickly stepped in to recycle these funds by borrowing from OPEC and lending to third world governments in Latin America and Africa.

【译文】商业银行迅速介入,通过向欧佩克借款再贷给拉美以及非洲的第三世界国家来使这些资金得到循环利用。

【解析】OPEC(欧佩克)是 Organization of Petroleum Exporting Countries(石油输出国组织)的简称,系石油输出国家为了对抗几个主要石油公司片面降低石油价格,而于 1961 年 1 月正式成立的组织。step in 是"干预,介入"的意思。borrow 和 lend 分别表示"借进"和"借出",这里把 borrow 译成"借",lend 译成"贷",使意思一目了然,不会造成歧义。

[3] Even Mexico, long thought to be highly creditworthy, announced that it could no longer service its $80 billion in international debt without an immediate new loan of $3 billion.

【译文】就连一直被认为信用度很高的墨西哥也宣称:除非能够立即获得一笔价值 30 亿美元的新贷款,否则将无力偿还所欠下的 800 亿美元国际债务。

【解析】creditworthy 意为"有信誉的,讲信用的"。service 这里作动词与 debt 连用,表示

"支付(债务或贷款的)利息",如:
The cash-based statement will provide information about a company's ability to service its debt.
现金收付制的报表将提供关于一家公司偿还债务能力的信息。

[4] ... an IMF-dictated series of macroeconomic policies were accepted by the Mexican government including tight control over the growth of the money supply and major cuts in government spending.

【译文】……墨西哥政府接受了国际货币基金组织规定的一系列宏观经济政策,其中包括严格控制货币供应增长和大量削减政府开支。

【解析】英语多使用被动语态,而汉语多用主动语态,翻译这个句子时就要根据目的语的表达习惯,即汉语的表达习惯,将被动语态化为主动语态。

[5] In April of that year the IMF endorsed a new approach first proposed by Nicholas Brady, US Secretary of the Treasury.

【译文】当年4月,国际货币基金组织认可了一项由美国财政部长尼古拉斯·布莱迪首先提出的解决债务问题的新方案。

【解析】endorse 在该句中是"支持;认可;赞同"的意思,所以 endorsed a new approach 意为"认可了一个新方案"。endorse 还有"背书;签署"的意思,如:
To endorse means to sign one's name as payee on the back of a note.
背书意味着作为受款人在票据的背面签字。
Secretary of the Treasury 指"财政部长"。译文中"解决债务问题的"部分属于增译,原句中并未指出,但是从上下文中可以知道这个新方法是为了解决债务问题而提出的,增译出原句中隐含的内容使汉语译文意思更加明确。

[6] The first application of the plan was the Mexican debt reduction of 1989 which cut that country's debt of $107 billion by about $15 billion.

【译文】1989年,墨西哥债务削减是该方案的首次实施,这次的削减将该国原先欠下的1070亿美元的债务减掉了近150亿美元。

【解析】这句中要注意 cut ... by ... 的翻译。cut ... by about $15 billion 意思是"减掉了近150亿美元",而不是"减到150亿美元";如果原句中是 cut ... to about $15 billion,那么就表示"减到了150亿美元"。

[7] It was obvious that loan conditions needed to extend beyond the project to the economy at large.

【译文】很明显,贷款的条件要从对具体项目有所限制扩展到对整个经济体做出要求。

【解析】the economy 这里指的是一个"经济体"。
at large 表示"整个",如 society at large 指"整个社会"。

[8] In addition to providing funds to support specific projects, the bank now provides loans for the government to use as it sees fit in return for promises on macroeconomic policy.

【译文】除了为具体项目提供资金,世界银行目前也向政府提供自认为是合适的贷款,只要这笔贷款能够换取该政府对宏观经济政策作出承诺。

【解析】 as it sees fit 中 it 指世界银行。
in return for 表示"作为……的报答"。

Passage B (English-Chinese Translation)

Currency Union: A Long-Term Vision?

Words & Expressions

Work on the following words and expressions and write the translated version in the space provided:

foreign competition	
financial intermediaries	
non-performing loans	
financial service business	
financial integration	
investors herd behaviour	
initiate institutional reforms	
amasse huge amounts of reserves	
productive investment	
the integrated global financial system	
emergency balance-of-payments support	
the international financial architecture	
financial and monetary integration	
synchronize business cycles	
financial liberalization	

The financial systems in the Asia-Pacific region are known to be unevenly developed, often bank-based, controlled by the State and closed to foreign competition. Banks and other financial intermediaries of these countries, including China and Japan, are saddled with large amounts of non-performing loans. Unless these bad loans are removed, they could pose a serious systematic risk for a country's financial system and expose it to financial crises.[1] China, Japan and the South-East Asian countries affected by the 1997 financial crisis are taking steps to deal with this issue.

Financial markets and financial service businesses are tightly regulated and closed to foreign investors and borrowers, thereby restricting cross-border financial transactions in the region.[2] The lack of financial integration has resulted in inefficient allocation of resources and has also rendered the region highly susceptible to financial instability caused by speculation, panic, mania and investors herd behaviour.[3]

A number of East Asian countries which suffered severe financial crises in 1997 – 1998 have taken steps to restructure their financial systems and have initiated institutional reforms, including reform of their legal and regulatory systems. However, despite these, the momentum of the reform efforts has to be intensified in order to improve the efficiency and the stability of the financial systems. These crisis-affected countries have amassed huge amounts of reserves for fighting future financial crises instead of strengthening their financial markets and institutions; at the same time investment in infrastructure and social and rural development has been less than desired. Some of the reserve holdings of Hong Kong of China, China; Japan; the Republic of Korea; and Taiwan Province of China could also be lent to other countries for their productive investment, but there are no channels to facilitate such lending. In a world economy that is being rapidly globalized, Asia-Pacific economies cannot remain much longer outside the integrated global financial system.[4] Therefore, one possible vision for the future of the financial sector is financial modernization and integration through financial reform and cooperation.

The idea of establishing an Asian monetary fund was first proposed by Japan in September 1997 following the Asian financial crisis. The original objective of such a fund was to make available a pool of funds to be quickly disbursed as a means of emergency balance-of-payments support for economies affected by the crisis.[5] Although many in the region welcomed the proposal, it failed to gain support from the United States and IMF on the grounds that it would weaken the role of IMF.

The proposal has recently met with some support from early opponents, as such a fund could play a complementary role to IMF by providing funds required in a crisis situation which IMF alone would not be able to galvanize. However, the realization of an Asian monetary fund would greatly depend on the region's ability to fit into the international financial architecture. Further, the linkages between the fund and IMF should be complementary and not competing arrangements.

Empirical studies invariably point to the large increase in intraregional trade in East Asia in recent years as a development conducive to financial and monetary integration in East Asia.[6] This increase has in turn served to synchronize business cycles across East Asian countries, thereby producing economic conditions that are favourable to the creation of a currency union in the region.

Against these trade and macroeconomic developments, financial liberalization throughout the region has led many countries to establish closer linkages with international financial markets than before, but not with markets of other neighbouring countries in the region.

In contrast, however, the financial markets of European countries were much more integrated with one another in the 1970s and 1980s than the markets of Asian countries are at present. With the increasing tendency towards regional cooperation in trade in Asia and the Pacific, better currency management and monetary and financial integration will become necessary.

Notes

[1]　Unless these bad loans are removed, they could pose a serious systematic risk for a country's financial system and expose it to financial crises.

【译文】除非这些坏账被消除，否则会给国家金融体系带来不可避免的严重风险，并有可能使之陷入金融危机。

【解析】systematic risk 意思是"不可避免的风险"，也译作"系统性风险"。当作"系统性风险"理解时，则与证券投资有关。投资于一种证券或一组证券的总风险是由系统性风险和非系统性风险（unsystematic risk）所构成的。所谓系统性风险是指由于整个市场情况变动所引起的风险，所谓非系统性风险则是指个别证券由于特殊原因所造成的风险。

expose ... to 意为"使遭受；使处于……的作用（或影响）之下"。

[2]　Financial markets and financial service businesses are tightly regulated and closed to foreign investors and borrowers, thereby restricting cross-border financial transactions in the region.

【译文】金融市场和金融服务业受到严格管制，而且不对外国投资者和借款人开放，从而限制了地区内的跨国金融交易。

【解析】be tightly regulated 意为"受到严格管制"。

[3]　... has also rendered the region highly susceptible to financial instability caused by speculation, panic, mania and investors herd behaviour.

【译文】而且使该地区极容易受到由投机、恐慌、狂热以及投资者羊群行为所引起的金融不稳定的影响。

【解析】susceptible 意为"易受影响的"；financial instability 意为"金融不稳定"。

speculation 意为"投机；投机买卖"；动词 speculate 意思是"做投机买卖"，如：

He speculated in foreign exchange and lost a lot of money.

他做外汇的投机买卖，损失了不少钱。

herd behaviour 译作"羊群行为，从众行为"，是金融市场中一种特殊的非理性行为，它是指投资者在信息环境不确定的情况下，行为受到其他投资者的影响，模仿他人决策，或者过度依赖于舆论（即市场中的压倒多数的观念），而不考虑自己的信息的行为。

[4]　In a world economy that is being rapidly globalized, Asia-Pacific economies cannot remain much longer outside the integrated global financial system.

【译文】世界经济正在迅速走向全球化，所以亚太经济体不可能长久处在一体化的全球金融体系之外。

【解析】动词 integrate 是"使成一体，使结合"的意思；integrated global financial system 意思是"一体化的全球金融系统"。

[5]　The original objective of such a fund was to make available a pool of funds to be

quickly disbursed as a means of emergency balance-of-payments support for economies affected by the crisis.

【译文】 建立这样一个基金的最初目的是为了在一些经济体受到危机影响的时候,能够有大量资金迅速用来支付紧急情况下的国际收支差额。

【解析】 a pool of funds 意为"大量资金"。

复数形式的 economies 这里表示"经济体"。

disburse 意为"支付,支出"。

emergency balance-of-payments support 意为"紧急国际收支援助"。

[6] Empirical studies invariably point to the large increase in intraregional trade in East Asia in recent years as a development conducive to financial and monetary integration in East Asia.

【译文】 实证研究指出,东亚近几年地区内贸易的大量增长有利于该地区金融和货币一体化的发展。

【解析】 intraregional trade 意思是"地区内的贸易",指限于地区内各国之间的贸易,而 interregional 则指"地区间的贸易"。

financial and monetary integration 译作"金融和货币一体化"。

conducive to 表示"有助于,有益于"。

Passage C (Chinese-English Translation)

通胀与调控

中国经济体系中,某些产业的发展非常迅速。在当前石油价格高涨的环境下,从通货膨胀的角度看,这些迅速发展的产业值得引起人们的注意和警惕。中国政府已经意识到了这一点。为了控制某些产业过度的增长,官方采取了渐进的调整手段,来避免因一系列宏观调控可能引起太过突然的变化。为此,政府首先是集中力量,对一些特别的产业进行调控,而不是针对整个经济。举例来说,政府并没有去提高整体的利率,而仅仅是提高了某些产业的利率,从而使得这一批借款人去承担较大的风险。这样的方式,可以使整个经济体维持正常的运作,而同时又合理地迫使这一些特殊产业削减它们的一些发展计划。

最重要的是,由于这种循序渐进的宏观调控方式,普通百姓们可以继续享受那些由经济快速发展所带来的一系列好处。

当然,谁也不敢百分之百保证这种渐进的调控手段会取得完全成功,但我个人认为,这是控制过度增长的一种正确方式。虽然一些外国银行和专家们经常会建议采取更为迅速的手段,但这样的做法确实存在着许多风险。

Translation Skills (Ⅱ)

被动语态的翻译

英语和汉语在语态上都有主动与被动之分。然而,英语和汉语分属两个完全不同的语系，因此差异较大。英语中被动语态使用范围很广，凡是不必说出主动者、不愿说出主动者、无法说出主动者或为了连贯上下文的场合，往往使用被动语态。汉语虽然也有被动语态，但使用范围较窄。英语被动语态有着固定模式，译成汉语时往往形式多样。英语被动句既可译成汉语被动句，也可译成主动句或者判断句。

一、译成汉语被动句

汉语中也有用被动语态表达的情况，但是汉语表示被动语态的标记比英语来得丰富多彩。在必须使用被动时，除了明显的"被"字外，汉语中还有许多字眼可以表示被动，常见的有："遭""受""由""给""叫""让""使""把""得到""蒙""靠""获""加以""予以""为……所""被……所"等，译者可酌情进行选择，以便更符合汉语习惯，避免所谓的"翻译腔"。

例：

（1）If the scheme is approved, the project will start immediately.
  如果方案被批准，将立即开工。

（2）The car was seriously damaged.
  这辆小汽车遭到严重的损坏。

（3）The reform and opening up policy is supported by the people all over the country.
  改革开放政策得到全国人民的支持。

（4）This project will be decided by the manager.
  这份计划将由经理决定。

（5）The plan of designing the workshop will be discussed tomorrow.
  设计车间的计划将在明天加以讨论。

（6）This matter must be discussed at the meeting.
  这件事必须在会上予以讨论。

（7）He was obsessed with fear of poverty.
  对贫困的担心使他忧虑重重。

（8）Although he introduced many improvements for this organization, his greatness was not recognized.
  虽然他为该公司做了多项技术改进工作，但他的卓越才能并未得到赏识。

（9）Some people hope that the resolution of the General Assembly will at last be respected by member states and by Israel in particular.
  一些人希望联合国大会的这项决议终将得到各会员国，尤其是以色列的尊重。

（10）Economic development is obtained by scientific advance.
  经济的发展是靠科技的进步取得的。

（11）Only 1/10,000 part of the energy radiated annually from the sun is taken up by plants.
  太阳每年辐射到地球的热量只有万分之一为植物所吸收。

二、译成汉语主动句

1. 保留原文主语

英语中一些被动结构的句子译成汉语时，原文中的主语仍然保留，译文中没有表示被动的标志，如"被""把"字等，形式上是主动句，但表达被动意义。

例：

（1）Most of the problems have been settled satisfactorily.

大部分问题已经圆满地解决了。

（2）Any business may be operated as a partnership.

任何企业都可以以合伙的方式经营。

（3）The money will be used to sustain national parks and reserves within the tropical rain forest belt, in countries around the globe.

这笔款将用于维持全世界范围内的国家公园和热带雨林地区保留林的发展。

2. 原文的主语在译文中作宾语

翻译时，可将原文的主语译成汉语里的宾语，而把原文的行为主体或相当于行为主体的介词宾语译成主语。

例：

（1）He is liked by all his friends.

他所有的朋友都喜欢他。

（2）Large quantities of chemical fertilizer are used by modern agriculture.

现代农业使用大量化肥。

3. 将原文中的某一部分转译成主语

被动句内含有地点状语或其他介词短语时，可先把这些状语（或一部分）译成汉语中的主语，再把原句中的主语译成宾语。

例：

（1）Communications satellites are used for international live transmission throughout the world.

全世界都知道通信卫星用于国际间的实况转播。（状语转译成主语）

（2）Mary was taught Chinese by Mr. Wang.

玛丽的汉语是王先生教的。（宾语转译成主语）

4. 增补主语

在翻译某些被动语态时，如果原句未包含动作的发出者，或原句中没有合适的词充当译文的主语，译成主动句时可从逻辑出发，适当添加泛指性主语，如"大家""人们""有人""我们"等，并把原句的主语译成宾语。

例：

（1）He will be considered a weak leader.

人们会认为他是一个能力差的领导。

（2）This lesson is considered very important for the young workers.

大家认为这堂课对青年工人很重要。

（3）Smoking is known to be harmful to health.

大家知道,吸烟有害健康。

5. 译成无主语句

英语的许多被动句不需要或无法讲出动作的发出者,翻译时往往可采用无主语句的形式来表达。一般来说,描述什么地方发生、存在或消失了什么事物的英语被动句,和表示看法、态度及告诫、要求、号召等的英语被动句,以及不带"by"短语并含有情态动词的被动句都可以采用这种译法。

例:

（1）Smoking is forbidden in public places.

公共场合禁止吸烟。

（2）Population growth must be controlled so that the economy can be developed.

必须控制人口增长,才能发展经济。

（3）Emphasis must be laid on the upgrading of product quality.

必须强调产品质量的不断改进。

（4）New sources of energy must be found to avoid causing energy shortages in the world.

必须找到新的能源,以避免造成世界上能源的短缺。

（5）To develop economy, different kinds of talented people should be organized. People of real ability should be especially promoted and given raise.

要发展经济应当组织使用各种各样的人才,对那些真正有本事的人在工资级别上可以破格提高。

除了以上几种情况外,在英文中有一些常用的以"it"作为形式主语的被动句型,在翻译这类句子时一般以主动句式译出,有的不加主语,有的则加上"人们""大家""有人"之类的不确定的主语。这里列举一些常见的这类被动句型及其习惯译法:

1）译成无主语的主动句

It is said that … 据说……

It is estimated that … 据估计……

It is supposed that … 据推测……

It is reported that … 据报道……

It is hoped that … 希望……

It is well known that … 众所周知……

It must be admitted that … 必须承认……

It must be pointed out that … 必须指出……

2）加上不确定的主语

It is believed that … 有人认为……

It will be said that … 有人会说……

It was told that … 有人曾经说……

三、译成判断句

汉语中常用"……是……的"的这一句式来说明人和事物的客观情况。这种结构在语义上往往具有被动含义,可以与英语中的被动结构相通。在翻译实践中,一般将英语中用来说明客观情况的被动句转译成汉语的这一句式。

例:
(1) These stone processing machines have been introduced from Italy for the newly established factory.

这些石材加工机器是为新建工厂而从意大利引进的。

(2) Most of the commodities in the US markets are manufactured by Chinese enterprises.

美国市场上的大部分商品是由中国企业生产的。

(3) The Alps were formed this way when Africa bashed into Europe 130 million years ago.

阿尔卑斯山脉就是这样在一亿三千万年前非洲板块猛烈撞上欧洲板块时形成的。

(4) Beijing is a fast-developing IT hub, and many companies are based in the city's hi-tech area, Zhongguancun.

北京是一个快速发展的IT中心,许多公司都是以这个城市的高科技区——中关村为大本营的。

总之,英语较多地使用被动句,汉语中虽然也有被动句,但使用主动句的频率更高。在翻译英语被动句的时候,我们可以译成汉语被动句,也可译成主动句或判断句。翻译时要根据句子的总体结构,灵活采用恰当的翻译方法,但是不管使用哪种方法,都要做到对原文表达的忠实和准确,并兼顾形式的连贯和流畅。

Translation Exercises

1. In addition, his liaison contacts expose the manager to external information to which his subordinates often lack access.
2. The object of speculation is to make a profit out of anticipated changes in exchange rates.
3. We should look at manufacturing and services as an integrated business.
4. Bonds can also be classified by the manner in which the related interest is disbursed.
5. 目前世界银行主要为较不发达国家提供资金。(finance)
6. 这家公司没有支付债务利息的现款。(service)
7. 他的申请已被委员会批准。(endorse)
8. 中国的经济发展不仅有益于自己,也有益于全世界。(at large)

Unit 5

Passage A (English-Chinese Translation)

Defining Risk

Words & Expressions

Work on the following words and expressions and write the translated version in the space provided:

money market fund	_____
savings account	_____
the stock market or the bond market	_____
credit crunches	_____
low-risk return	_____
broad asset classes	_____
risk premiums	_____
treasury bills	_____
term premium	_____
specific risk	_____
a stock-picker	_____
no inherent reward	_____
diversified portfolios	_____

Risk means that we do not know what is going to happen, even though we occasionally have a good idea of the range of possibilities that we face. Investors face two distinct kinds of risk, and recognizing the difference between them is critically important.

"Systematic" risk is the risk that none of us can avoid if we are seeking returns higher than we would earn in a money market fund or a savings account. [1] Once we decide to go into the stock market or the bond market, or buy a piece of real estate, or buy a share of a privately owned business, we face the risks that are inherent to those types of investments—such as the vagaries of business activity, inflation, overvaluation, credit crunches, and foreign exchange crises. These are risks you cannot avoid if you are going to invest at all.

Investors will refuse to take these risks unless they expect a return greater than the low-risk return of cash or cash substitutes. In general, then, the expected returns on the broad asset classes bear some kind of systematic relationship to the risks as investors perceive them. These higher expected returns are known as "risk premiums". For example, the difference between the expected return on stocks and the expected return on bonds is known as the "equity risk premium"; the difference between the expected return on long-term bonds and 90-day treasury bills is called the "term premium". When investors are gloomy or frightened by the economic environment, equities will tend to have a higher expected return than times when everyone is optimistic and stocks are priced way up; the equity risk premium, therefore, varies directly with the fear or greed in the marketplace. [2]

What about the investor who decides to put 75 percent of a portfolio in automobile stocks or technology stocks? This investor is taking a risk over and beyond the risk of being in the stock market, because the market as a whole might go up a lot more, or go down a lot less, than these specific choices. This investor, in other words, has taken on "specific" risk in addition to systematic risk. But specific risk is avoidable. The investor can always hold a diversified portfolio with a risk that is no greater than the risk of market as a whole. [3] Hence, the investor who decides to be a stock-picker cannot expect to be rewarded simply for passing up the opportunity of being diversified and taking on specific risk instead. [4]

We can think of this in another way. No one will go into the stock market unless the stock market appears to offer a return greater than the return to be earned by holding cash. It has to be a positive-sum game, or no one will play, and stock prices will fall until the expected returns are appropriate to the risks involved. Stock-picking is a zero-sum game—if one investor is right to buy Stock A, the seller has to be wrong. Thus, stock-picking has no inherent reward for investors in the same way that the market as a whole incorporates an expected reward. [5]

One of the real attractions of international investing is that the systematic risk of investing in one market—say, the American market—can be reduced significantly by diversifying the investor's portfolio across many different markets. In other words, the systematic risk facing well-diversified global investors is less than the systematic risk they would face if confined to just one national market. [6]

Many investment managers devote their time and energy to seeking out profitable investments from which they hope to earn more than the equity premium return offered by the overall market (the increment of expected reward for investing in widely diversified portfolios that are structured to diversify away all specific risk and all extra-market risk). They operate on the belief that they know more than the sellers from whom they buy—and therefore will be able to buy low. Or when they are selling, they will know more than the buyers to whom they sell—and therefore will be able to sell high. This may have been realistic for numerous investors many years ago, but it is a more questionable strategy in today's market where the prices of stocks are set by the trading of sophisticated, informed, professional investors managing the funds of large institutions.

Notes

[1]　"Systematic" risk is the risk that none of us can avoid if we are seeking returns higher than we would earn in a money market fund or a savings account.

【译文】如果我们在寻求高于通过货币市场和储蓄账户所获利润的盈利,那我们将面临一种无法避免的风险,这种风险就叫作"系统性"风险。

【解析】systematic risk 是"系统性风险;不可避免的风险"。参见 Unit 4, Passage B, Note [1]。

[2]　When investors are gloomy or frightened by the economic environment, equities will tend to have a higher expected return than times when everyone is optimistic and stocks are priced way up; the equity risk premium, therefore, varies directly with the fear or greed in the marketplace.

【译文】当投资者因经济环境很悲观或者恐慌时,股票将带来的预期利润趋向于比当人们都很乐观而且股价上涨的时候要高。因此,股权风险溢价会直接随着市场中的恐惧和贪婪而变化。

【解析】句中含有较多专业术语,如 risk premium 译为"风险差额,风险酬金,风险溢价", equity risk premium 译为"股权风险溢价"。

[3]　The investor can always hold a diversified portfolio with a risk that is no greater than the risk of market as a whole.

【译文】投资者总是可以持有形形色色的投资组合,这样的投资组合所含的风险不会超过整个市场所含的风险。

【解析】portfolio 译为"投资组合(如债券和股票)",相关的术语有 portfolio investment(有价证券投资), investment portfolio(有价证券投资清单,有价证券投资组合/搭配)。no greater than 意为"不会超过,不会大于"。

[4]　Hence, the investor who decides to be a stock-picker cannot expect to be rewarded simply for passing up the opportunity of being diversified and taking on specific risk instead.

【译文】因此,决定成为股票挑选人的投资者无法期待仅仅因为放弃多样投资组合的机会,并且承担特殊风险,从而获得回报。

【解析】stock-picker 指的是"股票挑选人,为别人挑选股票的公司或专家",相关的术语有 stockbroker(证券经纪人), stockholder(股票持有者); pass up 译为"放弃;放过"; specific risk 译为"特殊风险",这种风险有时也叫作 unsystematic risk(非系统性风险),是一种仅影响少数资产的风险。

[5] Thus, stock-picking has no inherent reward for investors in the same way that the market as a whole incorporates an expected reward.

【译文】因此，挑选股票对于投资者而言不存在固有的回报，正如整个股票市场会产生预期的回报一样。

【解析】inherent 意为"内在的；固有的，与生俱来的"；in the same way that ... 译为"正如……一样"。

[6] In other words, the systematic risk facing well-diversified global investors is less than the systematic risk they would face if confined to just one national market.

【译文】换句话说，面向全球进行多样投资的投资者所面临的系统性风险不会大于他们局限在国内市场进行投资时所要面临的风险。

【解析】be confined to 译为"局限于……"。

Passage B (English-Chinese Translation)

Risk Adjusted
Stephen Roach

Words & Expressions

Work on the following words and expressions and write the translated version in the space provided:

asset prices	_____
ultra-loose monetary policy	_____
slower expansion of the money supply	_____
core inflation gauges	_____
global liquidity	_____
demand for commodities and components	_____
heightened geopolitical tensions	_____
borrow against one's homes	_____
housing market	_____
ward off unexpected blows	_____
temper worrisome global imbalances	_____
act as a bulwark against calamity	_____

With easy money harder to come by, investors must adopt a new safety code.

Financial markets have had the wind at their backs for the last few years.[1] Historically low interest rates, the economic rise of China, India, Russia and Brazil, and consistently strong corporate earnings made for heady increases in stock and commodities markets around the world. This has created the illusion that just about any bet—even the risky ones such as sugar futures and Indian pharmaceutical companies—was bound to pay off handsomely. Since May, that optimism has been challenged. Today asset prices are being weighed down by two powerful forces: monetary policy and geopolitical angst. This spells "risk reduction" for most investors—a far cry from the "risk-hungry" investment strategies that have worked so well over the past several years. [2]

Why is there the sudden concern about risk? One factor is that central banks are finally coming to their senses. After more than five years of ultra-loose monetary policy, the world's major monetary authorities are all on the tightening side of the policy equation for the first time since the early 1990s. As a result, interest rates are going up, setting the stage for slower expansion of the money supply. [3] This is occurring for two reasons. First, central banks are now satisfied that deflation has been avoided—an especially big deal for the Bank of Japan, which just abandoned nearly six years of zero interest rates. Second, authorities are concerned about the risks of incipient inflation. So-called core inflation gauges have accelerated in a climate of sharply rising energy prices. Determined to avoid the mistakes of the 1970s, central banks have been quick to tighten in response.

This changes the rules of engagement for investors, who are now being denied access to the cheap funds they were putting to work chasing higher-yielding investments in emerging markets or subprime corporate debt. [4] Indeed, stocks and bonds in emerging markets, which soared when money was plentiful, now stand to lose the most—and not just because global liquidity is returning to normal. There is also a chance that a likely slowdown in US consumer demand would crimp the economies of export-led developing countries. [5] China and Mexico would be especially vulnerable, as would the rest of an increasingly China-centric Asian supply chain. Nor has the developing world become more self-sufficient. While pan-Asian trade has increased significantly since the late 1990s, much of the trade is driven by demand for commodities and components to feed China's factories—which in turn rely heavily upon the US as the consumer of last resort.

Heightened geopolitical tensions could compound the risks in the markets. The rapidly escalating conflict in the Middle East, along with DPRK's missile crisis and another terrorist attack in India, has already led to a ratcheting up of oil prices. Higher oil prices, bad for business everywhere, may be particularly damaging right now. That's because they place another burden—more expensive gasoline and utility charges—on US consumers, who are short of savings and unable to sustain their spending by borrowing against their homes in a weakening housing market. This spells trouble for a global economy still overly dependent on the US consumer. [6]

That's not to say the world lacks resilience against geopolitical shocks. Morgan Stanley estimates global GDP will grow 4.7% this year. That's 40% faster than the 3.4% average gains in the pre-oil-shock years of 1979 and 1990. Strong growth provides an important cushion to ward off unexpected blows. At the same time, the so-called stewards of globalization—namely, the G-7, the IMF and the world's major central banks—are now focused on implementing policies that would temper worrisome global imbalances.

But we can no longer count on an abundance of cheap money sloshing around the world to act as a bulwark against calamity and push asset prices higher. Financial market conditions today are more treacherous, margins for error are smaller, and even if there is a miraculous resolution of current geopolitical tensions any sigh of relief by investors is likely to be fleeting. [7] The days of making easy money on risky assets are behind us.

Notes

[1]　Financial markets have had the wind at their backs for the last few years.

【译文】金融市场在过去几年里一直有股力量在推动其发展。

【解析】wind 意为"(驱人行动或驱事发展的)力量"。

at one's back 意为"作某人后盾,给某人撑腰",如:

He has the whole country at his back.

他有全国人民作后盾。

[2]　This spells "risk reduction" for most investors—a far cry from the "risk-hungry" investment strategies that have worked so well over the past several years.

【译文】这对于多数投资者而言意味着要"减少风险",这与多年来运行良好的"渴求风险"投资战略是大相径庭的。

【解析】spell 在这里作"招致;意味着"讲;risk reduction 和 risk-hungry 是两个反义短语;a far cry from sth. 是一个固定短语,意为"与……相去甚远,与……大相径庭"。

[3]　As a result, interest rates are going up, setting the stage for slower expansion of the money supply.

【译文】因此,利率正在上升,这是在为货币供应的减速膨胀作铺垫。

【解析】set the stage for ... 的意思是"为……做好准备或创造条件"。

[4]　This changes the rules of engagement for investors, who are now being denied access to the cheap funds they were putting to work chasing higher-yielding investments in emerging markets or subprime corporate debt.

【译文】这改变了向投资者所承诺过的规定,这些投资者现在已经不能获得低利率的资金来追求在新兴市场和次要公司债券中的高收益投资。

【解析】access 意思是"(使用某物或接近某人的)机会或权利",一般用 get/have access to ...;文中的 be denied access to ... 可译为"不再有……权利/机会";high-yielding investment 意思是"高收益投资";subprime 意思是"次重要的"。

[5]　There is also a chance that a likely slowdown in US consumer demand would crimp the economies of export-led developing countries.

【译文】美国可能减慢的消费者需求也有可能会阻碍以出口为主的发展中国家的经济发展。

【解析】 在 Unit 2 讲述定语从句的翻译技巧时,曾讲到含有 there be 的定语从句一般可采用融合法,也就是利用从句的关系代词与主句某成分的代替关系,根据意思重新组成汉语单句。本句即采用了此翻译方法。

[6] This spells trouble for a global economy still overly dependent on the US consumer.

【译文】 这对于过多依赖于美国消费者的全球经济意味着一种麻烦。

【解析】 overly 意为"过多地,过度地";be dependent on 意为"依赖,依靠"。

[7] Financial market conditions today are more treacherous, margins for error are smaller, and even if there is a miraculous resolution of current geopolitical tensions any sigh of relief by investors is likely to be fleeting.

【译文】 金融市场的条件越来越不可靠,误差幅度越来越小,即使对于当前的地缘政治紧张局势有奇迹般的解决措施,投资者如释重负的感觉也可能稍纵即逝。

【解析】 句中 margin for error 译为"误差幅度",再如 margin of profitability(盈利幅度)等;geo- 表示"地球,土地"之义,因此 geopolitical 译为"地理政治学的或地缘政治学的",再比如,geobiology(地理生物学),geochemistry(地球化学),geodynamics(地球动力学)等。

Passage C (Chinese-English Translation)

投机——让人欲罢不能

不断地在金融市场上投机操作是否可以使一个人真正获利,实在是令人怀疑。我们会说,一个幸运投机者可以毕生就只下一次大赌注,赚到了钱,然后功成身退、金盆洗手。但这种说法在逻辑上有两个问题:

首先,一旦投机者第一次尝到了这么大的甜头,他就会认为他一定也会有第二次、第三次的好运,所以他一定会再次下赌注。而事实上,如此好运接踵而至的可能性实在太小了,最终的惨败则是不可避免的。

其次,就是很少真正有人可以在第一次就能幸运地赚到一大笔钱。而在时来运转、找到自己的"幸运"之前,他们就都已经是损失惨重了。但是,大家也都知道,市场上的投机活动却从来也不曾停止过。

不可否认,世界各国的经济在最近一段时间内的强劲增长是导致原油价格上扬的主要因素之一,但是对冲基金在短时间内大量购买原油期货也是另一个很重要的原因。然而,原油价格上涨并不是一件孤立的事情,它同时也给市场带来了新的机会,这时新的投机者们也就随之姗姗入场了。

Translation Exercises

1. Investment portfolio is actually the whole lot of bonds and stocks involved in investments made by a company.
2. Portfolio investment means investment in stocks, bonds, and other securities in

contrast to direct investment.
3. Attitudes towards daydreaming are changing in much the same way in which attitudes towards night dreaming have changed.
4. Multinational enterprises are different from companies that confine their activities to the domestic market in that MNEs do not see the company as confined to its local roots.
5. 农场生活与我已过惯的日子迥然不同。(a far cry from sth.)
6. 本周末两国领导人之间的会谈将有助于和平协议的达成。(set the stage for)
7. 如今我们有很多方式可以获取信息。(access)
8. 我们希望有外援,但我们不能依赖外援。(be dependent on)

Passage A (English-Chinese Translation)

An Attempt to Estimate China's Bad Loans Backfires

Words & Expressions

Work on the following words and expressions and write the translated version in the space provided:

auditing and consulting firm
the latest government estimate
state-owned banks
the official tally
Ernst & Young
a revised version
in due course
savage reaction
range from ... to ...
stockmarket listing
categorical withdrawal
credit surge
balance sheets
rational lenders

    Although China likes most of its numbers to be big, it has been trying to reduce one of them: the size of the bad loans burdening its banks. A report this month by Ernst & Young, a big auditing and consulting firm, therefore came as quite a shock. Ernst & Young, which does plenty of work on the mainland, claimed that China's stock of non-performing loans (NPLs) added up to $911 billion. This is more than five-and-a-half times the latest government estimate of $164 billion, published in March. The report deemed the country's big four state-owned banks, which are trying to attract international investors, to be carrying $358 billion of bad loans, almost three times the official tally.

The People's Bank of China, the country's central bank, quickly attacked the research as "ridiculous and barely understandable". This week an embarrassed Ernst & Young withdrew it, admitting that it was "factually erroneous" and that it had somehow slipped through the firm's normal checks. Ernst & Young says it plans to publish a revised version in due course.

The authorities' savage reaction is easy to understand. Other commentators and consultants have published estimates of China's NPLs ranging from $300 billion to $500 billion without attracting similar condemnation. Ernst & Young's estimate stood out not only for its size but also for its timing. [1] The central bank's rebuttal came on the very day that Bank of China, the second of the big four to attempt a stockmarket listing in Hong Kong, began its investor road show. [2] Bank of China plans to raise $9.9 billion, even more than the $9.2 billion pulled in by China Construction Bank, which was floated last October. A third big bank, Industrial and Commercial Bank of China, hopes for $10 billion in September. Awkwardly, Ernst & Young is this institution's auditor.

Even so, the firm's categorical withdrawal of its research looks like an overreaction. The report was more than a compilation of historic bad debts; drawing on work by other organizations, it also made a stab at estimating the new NPLs that will result from a lending spree between 2002 and 2004. [3] These account for most of the difference between Ernst & Young's figures and the official ones. And they are particularly relevant now that the mainland is in the midst of another credit surge: new loans in April amounted to 317 billion yuan ($40 billion), more than twice as much as in the same month last year. Although China has made progress in shifting bad loans off the banks' balance sheets, there is little sign that the banks themselves have fundamentally changed their behaviour and become rational lenders.

Neither side emerges with much credit from this episode. [4] Ernst & Young seems to have caved in too quickly to Chinese demands, at a cost to the perceived independence that it needs to win respect and clients. [5] The Chinese authorities, meanwhile, look like bullies. Bad loans are almost certainly greater than the official numbers say, even if they are less than Ernst & Young's estimate. To deny this is naive and damages the credibility needed to sell NPLs and shares in its banks to foreign investors. These, indeed, may turn out to be the only winners, if the tale reminds them of the real state of Chinese banks as another one passes round the hat. [6]

Notes

[1]　Ernst & Young's estimate stood out not only for its size but also for its timing.

【译文】而安永的估计不仅是在数额上,更重要的是在发表的时机上触怒了当局。

【解析】Ernst & Young 公司是世界著名的四大会计师事务所之一,中文译名为"安永"。其他三所分别为 Price Waterhouse Coopers (PWC),中文名为"普华永道";Klynveld Peat Marwick Geordeler (KPMG),中文名为"毕马威";Deloitte & Touche

(DTT),中文名为"德勤"。

这个句子中 estimate 作名词,是"估计,估算"的意思。上文提到安永公司对中国不良贷款总额的估算为9110亿美元,而中国官方记录只有1640亿美元,安永的估算远远超过官方数字,所以让当局很难堪。该句中 stand out 这个短语原是"醒目,突出"的意思,这里由"醒目"引申到"触怒了当局"。

[2] The central bank's rebuttal came on the very day that Bank of China, the second of the big four to attempt a stockmarket listing in Hong Kong, began its investor road show.

【译文】央行的反驳正是在四大国有银行中的第二大银行——中国银行准备为在香港上市而进行路演的时候提出的。

【解析】文章第一段也提到过 the country's big four state-owned banks(中国四大国有银行),这四大银行分别指中国工商银行(Industrial and Commercial Bank of China)、中国银行(Bank of China)、中国建设银行(China Construction Bank)和中国农业银行(Agricultural Bank of China)。the central bank 即指中国的央行——中国人民银行(The People's Bank of China)。

listing 这里指"(股票的)上市",如:

If a company gains a listing on the Stock Exchange, this will provide the long-term opportunity of raising capital by issuing fresh shares.

如果一家公司在股票交易所上市,这给它提供了通过发行新股筹资的长远机缘。

[3] The report was more than a compilation of historic bad debts; drawing on work by other organizations, it also made a stab at estimating the new NPLs that will result from a lending spree between 2002 and 2004.

【译文】这份报告不仅是一本历史坏账的汇编,在利用其他机构研究的基础上,它还试图估计出新的不良贷款将主要来源于2002至2004年间的放贷热潮。

【解析】drawing on work by other organizations 中的 draw on 是"动用;利用"的意思。

make a stab at 或 take (have) a stab at 是"试图做,尝试"的意思,如:

Even if you've never done it before, make a stab at it.

即使你从未做过,不妨试一下吧。

NPLs 是 non-performing loans 的缩写。

spree 原意是"无节制的狂热行为";lending spree 这里译作"放贷热潮"。

[4] Neither side emerges with much credit from this episode.

【译文】在这一事件中,双方都没有表现出更多的可信性。

【解析】episode 原本指"一段情节;一个插曲",这个句子里实际是指上文提到的整个事件。

[5] Ernst & Young seems to have caved in too quickly to Chinese demands, at a cost to the perceived independence that it needs to win respect and clients.

【译文】安永似乎过于迅速地屈服于中国的要求,代价是丧失了其赖以赢得尊重和客户的独立性。

【解析】cave in 是"投降,屈服"的意思。

[6] These, indeed, may turn out to be the only winners, if the tale reminds them of

the real state of Chinese banks as another one passes round the hat.

【译文】确实,唯一的赢家或许会是这些外国投资者,因为如果下次再有人想要圈钱的话,这个故事将会提醒投资者了解中国这些银行的真实状况。

【解析】reminds them 中的 them 指的是投资者。

pass round the hat 或 pass the hat（round）意为"募捐",在这里含有贬义,翻译成"圈钱"是因为前文中提到投资者了解到银行不可信,所以银行向他们募股时,在他们眼里可能带有欺骗性质。

Passage B (English-Chinese Translation)

China's Reserves: A Money Machine

Words & Expressions

Work on the following words and expressions and write the translated version in the space provided:

boost the return _____
foreign-exchange reserves _____
higher yielding equities and commodities _____
state investment agency _____
fund manager _____
Standard Chartered _____
dollar reserves _____
euro-denominated reserves _____
excessive liquidity _____
exchange-rate regime _____

China wants to boost the return that it earns on its $1 trillion-plus stash of foreign-exchange reserves. The Prime Minister, Wen Jiabao, said on January 20th that the country would explore new ways of investing the money, which is held mostly in liquid American government securities.[1] But his statement was vague. It could simply imply broadening the composition of assets held by the People's Bank of China (PBOC) to include higher yielding equities and commodities; or, more dramatically, part of the reserves could be transferred to a separate state investment agency which would maximize returns like a fund manager.[2]

Even as things stand, the PBOC is earning a handsome profit. According to Stephen Green, an economist at Standard Chartered, it made a profit of $29 billion last year—more than any of the world's commercial banks.

Much attention has been given to the large losses that the PBOC could suffer if the yuan rose sharply against the dollar (in which around 70% of reserves are held).[3] Last year, the loss on its dollar reserves, as a result of a modest rise in the yuan, was partially offset by a gain on its euro-denominated reserves as the euro strengthened. Mr Green estimates that, overall, the bank suffered a balance-sheet loss of 26 billion yuan ($3.3 billion) because of currency movements.

However, this loss was dwarfed by the PBOC's net interest income.[4] It earned an estimated 343 billion yuan on its foreign reserves last year. On the other side of the ledger it had to pay interest of 90 billion yuan on banks' reserves held at the central bank and on bills it issued to absorb excessive liquidity (largely caused by the surge in foreign exchange reserves).[5] Putting this with the foreign-exchange loss gives a total profit for 2006 of 227 billion yuan, or $29 billion. Citigroup and Bank of America, the world's most profitable banks, each made net profits of just over $21 billion in 2006.

The PBOC's earnings are vast partly because the interest rate it pays on its own bills is much lower than American interest rates, so it makes money from mopping up the liquidity created by an increase in reserves. This means that as long as American rates remain above those in China, today's exchange-rate regime—of buying dollars to hold down the yuan—will remain profitable.[6]

Notes

[1]　… that the country would explore new ways of investing the money, which is held mostly in liquid American government securities.

【译文】……国家将寻求新的外汇储备投资方式,目前大部分的外汇储备用以购买美国政府的流动证券。

【解析】这里 the money 指上一句中提到的 foreign-exchange reserves,因此将本句中的 the money 翻译成"外汇储备"。securities 意为"有价证券",始终为复数形式,其包括股票(stock certificate)、债券(bond)。government securities(政府证券)又称 treasury securities(国库证券),根据国库证券期限的长短,可分为国库券(treasury bills)、国库中期债券(treasury notes)及国库长期债券(treasury bond)三种。

[2]　… or, more dramatically, part of the reserves could be transferred to a separate state investment agency which would maximize returns like a fund manager.

【译文】……或者,还有一种更戏剧化的说法,即部分储备会被转移到一家独立的国家投资机构,该机构可以像基金管理人一样使利润获得最大化。

【解析】这个句子及省略号部分是对前一句的两种猜测,所以翻译 more dramatically 时,增译为"更戏剧化的说法",使意义更加明确。

a separate state investment agency 是指"独立的国家投资机构"。

[3]　Much attention has been given to the large losses that the PBOC could suffer if the yuan rose sharply against the dollar (in which around 70% of reserves are held).

【译文】 许多人都在关注如果人民币对美元的汇率迅速上升将可能给中国人民银行带来的巨大损失,因为(中国)所持有的外汇储备中有70%是美元。

【解析】 the yuan rose sharply against the dollar 这里译为"人民币对美元的汇率迅速上升"。

原句尾括号中是补充说明的成分,翻译成汉语时可以作为原因,解释为什么人民币对美元的汇率迅速上升会给中国人民银行带来巨大损失。

[4] However, this loss was dwarfed by the PBOC's net interest income.

【译文】 但是,中国人民银行的净利息收益远远超过了这笔损失。

【解析】 dwarf 意为"使显得矮小;使相形见绌"。原句使用的是被动语态,为了使译文符合汉语表达习惯,这里译作了主动语态。

[5] On the other side of the ledger it had to pay interest of 90 billion yuan on banks' reserves held at the central bank and on bills it issued to absorb excessive liquidity (largely caused by the surge in foreign exchange reserves).

【译文】 从分类账本的借方可以看出,中国人民银行还必须支付900亿元的利息,一是支付(各商业银行)存储在中央银行的存款准备金利息,二是支付其为吸收主要由外汇储备激增所引起的过多流动性而发行的票据的利息。

【解析】 本句的翻译适当使用了增词法,即将 banks 翻译成"各商业银行"以示与"中央银行"的区别;这样做既符合上下文意思,同时也避免了将 banks 简单译成"银行"可能导致的含混不清状况。ledger 是指会计业务中的"分类账",即将业务中的货币交易记录下来的账本,分借方和贷方。On the other side of the ledger 实际上是指在分类账本的借方,即记载了中国人民银行需要对外支付的款项的一方,所以这里译作"从分类账本的借方可以看出"。

[6] This means that as long as American rates remain above those in China, today's exchange-rate regime—of buying dollars to hold down the yuan—will remain profitable.

【译文】 这意味着只要美国利率一直高于中国利率,现今这种购入美元牵制人民币的汇率体制将仍然有利可图。

【解析】 hold down 意为"牵制,压制",regime 是"体制,体系"的意思,如 establish a new industrial regime(建立新的工业体制)。

Passage C (Chinese-English Translation)

采取积极有效措施,促进国际收支基本平衡

促进国际收支基本平衡,是贯彻落实科学发展观、实现经济全面协调可持续发展的内在要求。这次人民币汇率改革对于平衡国际收支、缓解外汇储备过快增长虽有裨益,但应该看到国际收支目前还不大可能很快基本平衡。实现国际收支的基本平衡需要加快经济结构的调整,转变经济增长方式,扩大国内需求,特别是居民消费需求的增长,并且应该采取积极有效的措施。

为此,特提出以下几点建议:一是在保持出口持续增长的同时扩大进口,缩小贸易顺差。要优化出口商品结构,严格控制高能耗、高污染产品的出口;扩大具有自主知识产权、自主品牌的商品出口,提高出口商品的质量和技术含量。要扩大国内短缺资源和战略原材料的进口,扩大先进技术和设备的进口。二是切实提高利用外资质量和效益,优化利用外资结构。引导外资更多地流向高新技术产业和中西部地区,促进国内产业调整和区域的协调发展;进一步开发服务市场,有序承接国际现代服务业转移。三是鼓励企业境外投资,大力支持有条件的企业"走出去",健全对境外投资的政策和协调机制。四是改革目前结售汇制度,逐步由强制性结汇向自愿结汇转变,将外汇逐步保留在企业,减少企业借外债的数量,同时也可减轻国家外汇储备增长过快的压力。五是分流出一部分多余的外汇,如从国家外汇储备中通过像中央汇金投资公司以投资形式充实国有商业银行资本金等。六是加强人民币汇率监测,改进国际收支统计手段和方法,提高对国际收支的分析和预警能力。

Translation Skills(Ⅲ)

增词法和减词法

英汉两种语言由于分属不同的语系,因此在语言结构、语法特点、表达习惯等方面都存在很大差异。英汉互译时,通常逐字逐词翻译是行不通的,译者必须根据原文的意思,上下文的逻辑关系,英汉两种语言不同的语法特点、表达习惯、所处的不同文化背景在译文中适当地增加或减少词语,以使译文能够忠实顺畅地表达原文的思想内容。增词法和减词法是英汉互译中不可缺少的技巧。

增词法是指在译文中增加一些原文字面上没有的词、词组,甚至句子,以便使译文意义更加完整、语法更加准确、逻辑更加清晰、表达更符合译入语语言习惯。一般而言,增词法在大的方面有两种情况:一是出于语义上的需要,把原文句子里"隐含"或上下文意思清楚而没有写出来的词在译文里补进去;另一种则是出于语法上的考虑,把原文中省略的句子成分补充进去。增词并不是可以无中生有地随意增加词,而应该增加原文中虽然没有表达出来但是意义隐含其中的一些词。

所谓减词法,就是在不影响原文整体意义的基础上,删除一些虽然原文中出现,但是没有必要在译文中表达出来的词语,以使译文简洁流畅,不会显得累赘。如果将英汉两种语言的词类进行比较,就能发现以下的情况:大部分词类如名词、动词、形容词等实义词是两种语言共有的,它们是翻译得以实现的基础;可是,英语中的一些往往不可或缺的虚词,如介词、冠词和连词,在汉语里有的出现频率极低,有的可有可无,有的甚至是多余的;少数系动词、代词也有这种现象。对于这些语言现象,翻译时要按照原意和汉语的表达习惯进行适当地处理,包括删减。当然,减词的前提是不能减义。增词和减词是一个事物的两个方面,如果一个句子在英译汉时需要增词,那么在汉译英时则需要减词,反之亦然。下文将通过大量例证具体说明增词和减词这两种翻译方法。

一、出于语义上的需要增减词

例1 We will help this region out of its backwardness.
译文:我们要帮助这一地区摆脱落后状况。

例 2　The present position and potentialities of this region justify optimism.

译文：该地区当前所处的地位及其发展前景有理由使人对它抱乐观的态度。

英语中常用一些形容词或动词派生出来的抽象名词表示具体的概念。翻译时为了使汉语译文更符合规范，可根据上下文在其后面添加适当的表示具体概念的范畴名词，如"工作""状态""局面""事业""制度""行为""态度""过程""作用""方法""现象""原理""情绪""活动"等，而汉译英时，这样的概念范畴往往用一个英语名词就能译出。

例 3　Bush's war popularity was to erode because of economic problems.

译文：由于种种经济问题，布什在海湾战争中树立起来的声望开始下降。

为了实现有效的沟通避免译文读者产生误会或理解困难，对原文中一些有关社会与文化的内容译者有时需要在译文中适当增加少量解释或介绍的词语。如该例 3 译成中文时中国读者可能并不清楚原文中的"war"具体指哪一场战争，所以增译成"海湾战争"就可以避免读者因不了解背景情况而产生误解。反之，将该句回译成英文时，如果读者对象了解英语国家的文化，知道这里的"war"特指"海湾战争"，则无需将"海湾"二字译出。

例 4　Don't take it seriously. I'm just making fun of you.

译文：不要认真嘛！我不过开开玩笑罢了。

汉语里有许多语气助词，如"的""吧""呢""啊""呀""嘛""吗""啦""了""罢了""而已"等。不同的语气助词可以发生不同的作用，英译汉时细心体会原文，增加一些汉语所特有的语气助词，可以更好地表达原作的意义和修辞色彩。而英语中的语气是通过句子结构来传递的，比如说祈使句、感叹句等，所以汉译英时无须感叹词也可从字里行间感受出句子的语气。

例 5　Some people think modern economics can just close the gates, but the movement of capital and ideas knows no borders.

译文：有些人认为现代经济就是关起门来自我经营，但是资本的流动和观念的传播，从来是无国界的。

例 6　Please expedite the L/C so that we may execute the order smoothly.

译文：请速开信用证，以便顺利执行订单。

某些句子在英语中，就原文的表达形式来看，逻辑上是通的，但在译成汉语时，若不加上适当的词，在逻辑上就显得欠缺一些，比如例 5，出于汉语逻辑上的考虑，翻译时加上"自我经营"，把隐含的意思充分表达出来，使该句形式上合乎思维规律，意义上顺理成章。而例 6 译成汉语时虽然减译了"we may"，句子依旧意思明确、简洁通顺、合乎逻辑。所以，翻译时必须根据不同的句子和上下文决定是否应该增减词语。

二、出于语法上的需要增减词

例 7　a full moon　一轮满月
　　　　a mouth　一张嘴
　　　　two copies　两份副本

英语中的数词与可数名词往往直接连用，它们之间没有量词，而汉语却往往要借助量词。因此英译汉时应根据汉语表达习惯恰当地增加表示其形状特征或材料的量词，而汉译英时则应该根据英语语法省略汉语中的量词。

例 8　Our crops often suffered heavy losses because of bad weather.

译文：过去我们的庄稼常因天气不好而遭受重大损失。

例 9　New varieties are appearing all the time.

译文：新的品种正在不断涌现。

例 10　Sunshine kills many forms of harmful bacteria.

译文：太阳光能杀死许多种有害的细菌。

英语动词的时态靠动词词形变化或加助动词来表示，而汉语动词没有词形变化，表达时态要靠汉语特有的时态助词或一些表示时间的词。因此，翻译完成时往往添加"曾""已经""过""了"，翻译过去时往往添加"过去""曾""了""当时"等，翻译进行时往往用"在""正在""着"，而翻译将来时往往用"将""就""要""会""便"，翻译一般现在时加译"能""能够""可以"等。在汉译英时直接通过变化英语动词的词形就可以表达句子的时态，汉语中的时态助词或表示时间的词无须翻译。

例 11　Reading makes a full man; conference a ready man; writing an exact man.

译文：读书使人充实，讨论使人敏捷，写作使人准确。

英语的并列句中通常省略重复的动词，而汉语则通过重复动词，构成排比句式，增强表达效果。

例 12　He is very tall. So are his brothers.

译文：他很高，他的兄弟们也很高。

例 13　Does the sun ever get dark during the day? It does so when the moon hides it.

译文：白天太阳会变暗吗？当月亮遮住太阳时，太阳会变暗。

在英语中，常常对重复部分用词代替，如用 it, that, those 等代词或 do, do so, so, neither, nor, as 等结构代替。英译汉时，为了意思明确或便于表达，将原文中被代替了的部分加以重复；汉译英时，汉语中重复的部分可减译成英语中的代词等。

例 14　现在我们处在一种很新的经济中，即服务经济中，各种关系比具体的产品更重要。

译文：We now live in a very new economy, a service economy, where relationships are becoming more important than physical products.

汉语重意合，多通过上下文和语序来表示句子和词组间的逻辑关系，一般很少使用连接词，而英语重形合，一般用连接词来表示上述关系。汉译英时，常常需要增补连词，否则句子结构就会出现语法错误；而英译汉时，为了句子结构紧凑，在不影响表意的前提下可以省略连接词。

由此可见，增词法和减词法作为两种重要的翻译技巧，是有一定规律可循的。翻译过程中适时地运用这两种技巧可以使文章意思表达得更清楚、更流畅、更地道。当然，无论使用增词法还是减词法，都必须忠实原文，在对原文有透彻理解的基础上，通过适当的增词或减词，使原文意义在译文中再现出来，以便读者充分理解原文以及使文章更具特色。

Translation Exercises

1. A bank also renders a variety of other services, such as buying and selling securities and insurance for its customers.

2. In the case of stocks which are listed on a stock exchange, the most recent price at which the shares were traded is regarded as the market value.
3. This paper deals with the nation's problems, ranging from runaway inflation to a lowering of literacy levels.
4. You will find it profitable to buy from us because the quality of our products is far better than that of other foreign makers in your district.
5. 出口大于进口必然会增加就业。(boost)
6. 据估计,他们的股票在一个月后会超过12.5美元一股。(estimate)
7. 政府不得不动用储备并向国外借款。(draw on)
8. 他为那个残疾儿童向周围群众募捐。(pass the hat round)

Unit 7

Passage A (English-Chinese Translation)

Are Markets Efficient?

Words & Expressions

Work on the following words and expressions and write the translated version in the space provided:

the investment world
two principal camps
advocates of inefficient markets
market pricing
passive management
investment performance
independent variables
subsequent market
asset returns
arbitrage away

  The investment world can be broken into two principal camps: those who believe that markets are efficient, and those who believe they are inefficient. The capital markets of today function primarily on the basis of trading among those who believe that markets are inefficient.[1] Advocates of inefficient markets believe that market pricing does not correctly reflect all available information. They seek mispricing in markets or in an individual asset that can lead to improved returns, with risk control as a secondary objective.[2] Advocates of efficient markets believe that pricing already reflects all publicly available information; this leads to a very strong bias in favor of "passive management", with a focus on risk control first and investment performance as a secondary (or even nonexistent) objective. There are even theoretic foundations for both schools of thought: Equilibrium models provide a theoretic basis for observed market behavior in the context of "efficient pricing", while behavioral finance suggests that mispricing is inherent in human behavior.[3]

Sound evidence is presented by both camps. Advocates of efficient markets point to the fact that many supposed demonstrations of market inefficiency are not statistically significant, and those that are statistically significant often vanish after receiving public scrutiny.[4] Those who suggest that markets are inefficient like to point to the many times highly significant relationships are found between various independent variables and subsequent market or asset returns.

What is often lacking in this dialogue is an acknowledgement of the obvious: It is possible (even likely) that markets are inefficient, that active management can potentially add value, but that the inefficiencies are neither simple nor static nor inexpensive to exploit. In other words, part of the nature of market inefficiencies is that they tend to disappear. This means that once a market inefficiency is isolated and becomes widely known, it should begin to diminish or disappear as more money pursues the same inefficiency.[5]

Indeed, essentially all categories of active management presume that markets are mispriced or inefficient. They presume to add value by investing in a market or an asset that is in some fashion mispriced. Yet any market inefficiency is inherently an arbitrage opportunity: If enough money pursues the same market inefficiency, it must disappear. It is reasonable to surmise that inefficiencies that are uncomfortable, that produce increased return at the cost of reduced comfort, should not attract enough investors to "arbitrage away" the opportunity.[6] Accordingly, these inefficiencies might be expected to offer long-term gains for the patient investor.

Notes

[1] The capital markets of today function primarily on the basis of trading among those who believe that markets are inefficient.

【译文】如今资本市场的运作主要基于那些认为市场无效的商家之间的交易。

【解析】capital 作"资本"讲,如 actual capital 意为"实际资本",capital goods 意为"资本货物",capital-intensive 意为"资本密集型的"。on the basis of ... 意思是"以……为基础"。

[2] They seek mispricing in markets or in an individual asset that can lead to improved returns, with risk control as a secondary objective.

【译文】他们寻求市场中或单个资产中错定的价格,这些错定的价格可以使他们获得更多的盈利,而将风险控制作为次要目标。

【解析】misprice 意为"给……错定价格,给……标错价格"。
secondary 意为"第二的;次要的",如 secondary industry(第二产业),secondary risks(二等风险);与之相对应的词是 primary(第一的;首要的),如 primary industry(第一产业),primary risks(头等风险,一级风险),但 primary data 意为"原始资料,原始数据,第一手资料"。
本句中的定语从句比较长,因此在翻译时将从句译成和主句并列的一个分句,放在主句之后,前后用逗号隔开,并且重复先行词。

[3]　… Equilibrium models provide a theoretic basis for observed market behavior in the context of "efficient pricing", while behavioral finance suggests that mispricing is inherent in human behavior.

【译文】……均衡模型为有效标价背景下的观察市场行为提供了理论基础,而行为金融学则提出标错价格是人类行为中所固有的。

【解析】equilibrium models 意为"均衡模型";context 本义是"上下文,语境",这里指"环境,背景",如:

In the context of the present economic crisis it seems unwise to lower taxes.

鉴于当前的经济危机,降低税率似乎不妥。

while 有轻微的转折,它所引出的从句与前面的主句形成对照。

[4]　Advocates of efficient markets point to the fact that many supposed demonstrations of market inefficiency are not statistically significant, and those that are statistically significant often vanish after receiving public scrutiny.

【译文】支持市场有效的一方指出,许多关于市场无效的假定论证在统计学上是无意义的,而那些在统计学上有意义的则通常在受到公众仔细审查后消失。

【解析】advocate 指的是"支持者,拥护者,提倡者",经常用来表示这个意思的词还有 proponent, supporter 等。statistically 意思是"统计地,统计学上地", statistics 则表示"统计学"。

efficient market 意为"有效市场"。所谓有效市场,是指其股票价格能根据信息的变动迅速调整的市场,因此从理论上讲,在充分获得所有信息的情况下,股票现期市场价格是对将来收益的最好判断。

[5]　This means that once a market inefficiency is isolated and becomes widely known, it should begin to diminish or disappear as more money pursues the same inefficiency.

【译文】也就是说,一旦市场的无效突显出来并且为大众所了解,那么随着更多的资金寻求同样的市场无效,这种市场无效就会开始减少或者消失。

【解析】isolate 本义是"隔绝,隔离;孤立",但在这句中如果译成了"一旦市场的无效被孤立出来",未免有些牵强,所以应把它译成"一旦市场的无效突显出来"。

[6]　It is reasonable to surmise that inefficiencies that are uncomfortable, that produce increased return at the cost of reduced comfort, should not attract enough investors to "arbitrage away" the opportunity.

【译文】我们有理由推测,令人感到不安、且以逐渐丧失安全感为代价而增加盈利的市场无效性不应该吸引足够多的投资者来利用这一机遇进行"套利"。

【解析】it is reasonable to surmise that … 译成"我们有理由推测……",这样整个句子结构比较清晰。at the cost of … 意为"以牺牲……为代价",其他相关短语有 at all costs(不惜任何代价), at cost(按成本价格)。

arbitrage 意思是"套汇,套利",如 currency arbitrage 意为"套汇", stock arbitrage 意为"套购证券;股票投机"。

Passage B (English-Chinese Translation)

Catching Market Waves
Marc Faber

Words & Expressions

Work on the following words and expressions and write the translated version in the space provided:

the recent plunge in commodities prices	_____
industrial commodities	_____
bull market	_____
Kondratieff Waves	_____
up cycle	_____
downward wave	_____
demand curve	_____
per capita consumption of raw material and energy	_____
ultra-expansionary monetary policies	_____
correction phase	_____
international tensions	_____

History suggests the sharp drop in commodities prices may not last too long.

The recent plunge in commodities prices has investors wondering whether a major bubble has burst.[1] But was there really ever a bubble? It is true that since their lows between 1998 and 2001, commodities and especially industrial commodities have been on a tear. Between 1998 and early 2006, crude oil rose from $11 per barrel to over $70, copper from 60 cents per pound to over $4, nickel from $5,000 per tonne to over $20,000, while gold went from $255 an ounce to over $700. But before deciding that the commodities bull market is over, investors should consider the following: commodity price cycles—also called Kondratieff Waves, named after an influential early 20th century Russian economist—play out over decades. From peak to peak or trough to trough they last 45 to 60 years, and within that span there are also up and down cycles lasting 22 to 30 years. The last up cycle peaked in 1974; the last downward wave lasted for more than 20 years. While it's true that commodity prices have soared since 2001, the rise may have only just begun. That's because real commodity prices (adjusted for inflation) were, in the 1999 – 2001 period, at the lowest level in 200 years. Today, commodities (with the exception of copper) still sell in real terms for about one third their 1970s peak.[2]

It's no secret why prices are rising. The rapid industrialization of China (and increasingly India) has shifted the demand curve, leading to permanently higher equilibrium prices. China, which absorbed 12% of global copper production in 2000, now takes in close to 22%. Yet per capita consumption of raw material and energy in China and India is still low. The average US citizen consumes 27 barrels of oil annually, Japanese and South Koreans 17 barrels. But annual per capita consumption in China and India is 1.7 and 0.8 barrels, respectively. That demand is only going to grow over the long term.

Commodities have also been boosted by the ultra-expansionary monetary policies pursued by the US and Japan. Since 2002 excess liquidity has driven up prices for all kinds of assets, including real estate, stocks, art and collectibles, leading to a huge amount of leveraged speculation.[3] However, most recently, global liquidity, while still expanding, is doing so at decelerating rates; that has led to a sell-off in equities and commodities. I would expect this correction to last another few months—until central banks around the world embark once again on monetary expansion.[4] In this correction phase it would not be surprising for commodity prices to decline from their recent peak by 30% to 50%. Copper prices would seem to be particularly vulnerable.

We've seen this happen before. During the last great commodity bull market, gold declined from $195 an ounce to $103 between December 1974 and August 1976 and then rose by 800% to reach a peak in 1980. Similarly, in the great equities bull market between 1982 and 2000, the Dow lost 40% from August to October 1987, before a sevenfold rise. Long-term bull markets are characterized by intermediate sharp corrections, and I have little doubt that the commodities bull market will, following the current correction, reassert itself, although price leadership may change from industrial commodities to precious metals and grains.[5]

One lesson from history is worth bearing in mind. Rising commodity prices have historically led to an increase in international tensions, as countries become concerned about reliable supplies of raw materials.[6] If those tensions lead to war, commodity prices can go ballistic. All major modern industrial-commodity price peaks were reached during wartime—whether it be the Napoleonic Wars, the US Civil War, World War I, or the Vietnam War. So celebrate rising commodity prices if you must, but remember where they sometimes lead.

Notes

[1]　The recent plunge in commodities prices has investors wondering whether a major bubble has burst.

【译文】最近商品价格的猛跌使得投资者怀疑是不是一个大的经济泡沫破裂了。

【解析】plunge 意为"猛跌",如:

Share prices plunged as a result of the gloomy economic forecast.
由于经济前景暗淡,因而股票价格暴跌。

[2] Today, commodities (with the exception of copper) still sell in real terms for about one-third their 1970s peak.

【译文】今天,所有的商品除了铜之外,实际上都还是以20世纪70年代高峰期价格的三分之一出售。

【解析】in ... terms 译为"在……方面,从……方面讲";real 译为"真实的,实际的",在译文中简单译为"实际上"。

[3] Since 2002 excess liquidity has driven up prices for all kinds of assets, including real estate, stocks, art and collectibles, leading to a huge amount of leveraged speculation.

【译文】自从2002年以来,过剩流动性使得各种资产的价格上涨,包括房地产、股票、艺术品和收藏品,从而导致了大量的融资投机买卖。

【解析】excess liquidity = excessive liquidity,意为"过剩流动性";leverage 作名词时意为"杠杆作用",而作动词时则是"利用信贷牟取高利,利用贷款投机"的意思;leveraged 可与其他词组成固定短语,如 leveraged buyout 意为"融资收买,融资买入;杠杆收购",leveraged lease 意为"融资租赁,杠杆租赁"。

[4] I would expect this correction to last another few months—until central banks around the world embark once again on monetary expansion.

【译文】我预期这个修正会再持续几个月,直到全球的中央银行再次着手货币扩张。

【解析】monetary expansion 意为"货币扩张",相关短语还有 monetary assets(货币资产),monetary circulation(货币流通),monetary fluctuation(货币波动)等。

[5] Long-term bull markets are characterized by intermediate sharp corrections, and I have little doubt that the commodities bull market will, following the current correction, reassert itself, although price leadership may change from industrial commodities to precious metals and grains.

【译文】长期牛市的特点表现为中间会出现急剧修正,我并不怀疑商品的牛市会随着现行的修正再次发威,尽管价格的领头羊将由工业商品转变为贵金属和谷物。

【解析】I have little doubt that ... 译为"我并不怀疑",因为 little 含否定意义。reassert oneself 意为"重申自己的权威",这里引申为"再次发威",符合上下文意思。

[6] Rising commodity prices have historically led to an increase in international tensions, as countries become concerned about reliable supplies of raw materials.

【译文】历史上,不断上升的商品价格曾导致国际紧张局势的加剧,因为各国都开始担心是否能得到可靠的原材料供应。

【解析】historically 译为"在历史上,从历史观点上说",因此翻译该句时,状语 historically 被提前,作为整个句子的时间状语;international tensions 意为"国际紧张局势"。

Passage C　(Chinese-English Translation)

市场与经济

国际贸易原理认为，与小国相比，在同样的收入水平上，大国有更多的国内贸易机会和更大的市场，这为大国的企业和经济增长提供了较大的发展空间。我国目前的人均经济规模虽不大，但人均经济集合起来，就成为庞大的经济体。这就是为什么新加坡、以色列虽然是发达国家，却不能成为经济大国，而我国虽属于发展中国家，却是世界第四大经济实体。由于有巨大的市场，东边不亮西边亮，一国就具有抗衡世界经济波动的能力；而且，即使没有国际竞争，通过国内竞争，也可以促进创新，有效合理地配置资源。通过国内贸易，特别是地区间的贸易，也能获得规模经济，降低国内生产成本，提升国际竞争力。

我们知道，区域经济一体化的主要目标是寻求更大的市场，而这个市场从本质上讲是"人口"。从这个角度讲，我国几乎任何一个省份都相当于一个或数个欧洲国家。长期以来，地方政府审批制造成了我国各地区工业结构相似。目前，我国中部和东部地区工业结构相似率为93.5%，西部和中部地区的相似率为97.9%。各省市在技术水平上大体相当，但在个别技术上又有比较优势的一个局面，同时各地区生产要素禀赋存在较大差异。因而，实现我国国内各地区市场统一，就如同在我国国内形成一个既是水平的又是垂直的区域经济一体化，并且是其最高阶段——完全经济一体化，包括政治体制统一，却不需要让渡国家权力。即使是当今经济一体化最成功的欧盟要实现完全经济一体化也是遥遥无期的。各地区技术水平相当为国内产业内贸易提供了条件，资源禀赋的地区差异和技术差异又为国内垂直分工和产业在国内转移提供了条件。这是中国独一无二的、得天独厚的绝对优势，是世界上任何其他区域经济一体化不可比拟的。

Translation Exercises

1. While proactiveness is well understood in military warfare, it tends to be easily overlooked in the context of business.
2. Someone who engages in arbitrage purchases securities in one market for immediate resale in another in the hope of profiting from the price differential.
3. Seasoned investment managers know that performance will often be improved by pursuing an unconventional and often uncomfortable strategy.
4. We must cherish experience acquired at the cost of blood.
5. 不要以貌取人。(on the basis of)
6. 我不怀疑他们有足够的人力。(I have little doubt that ...)
7. 就你的建议而言，我们觉得还有改进的地方。(in terms of ...)
8. 我们的商品价格公道，品质优良。(reasonable)

Passage A (English-Chinese Translation)

Strategic Market Management
David A. AAKER

Words & Expressions

Work on the following words and expressions and write the translated version in the space provided:

planning cycle	_____
continuous, real-time information system	_____
periodic analysis	_____
develop strategic flexibility	_____
an emerging consumer-interest area	_____
a clear and shared understanding	_____
a distinctive and farsighted view	_____
regenerate core strategies	_____
reengineer core processes	_____
be out in front rather than catching up	_____
the projection-based approach	_____
long-range planning	_____
adapt strategic decision making to real time	_____

Strategic market management, or simply, strategic management, is motivated by the assumption that the planning cycle is inadequate to deal with the rapid rate of change that can occur in a firm's external environment. To cope with strategic surprises and fast-developing threats and opportunities, strategic decisions need to be precipitated and made outside the planning cycle.[1]

Recognition of the demands of a rapidly changing environment has stimulated the development or increased use of methods, systems, and options that are responsive. In particular, it suggests a need for continuous, real-time information systems rather than, or in addition to, periodic analysis.[2] More sensitive environmental scanning, the identification and continuous monitoring of information-need areas, efforts to develop strategic flexibility, and the enhancement of the entrepreneurial thrust of the organization may be helpful.[3] An information-need area is an area of uncertainty that will affect strategy, such as an emerging consumer-interest area. Strategic flexibility involves strategic options that allow quick and appropriate responses to sudden changes in the environment.

Strategic market management is proactive and future-oriented. Rather than simply accepting the environment as given, with the strategic role confined to adaptation and reaction, strategy may be proactive, affecting environmental change.[4] Thus, governmental policies, customer needs, and technological developments can be influenced—and perhaps even controlled—with creative, active strategies.

Some experts argue that managers should have a clear and shared understanding of how their industry may be different in 10 years and a strategy for competing in that world. They challenge managers to evaluate the extent to which

- Management has a distinctive and farsighted view, rather than a conventional and reactive view, about the future.
- Senior management focuses on regenerating core strategies rather than on reengineering core processes.
- Competitors view the company as a rule maker rather than a rule follower.
- The company's strength is in innovation and growth rather than in operational efficiency.

The company is mostly out in front rather than catching up.[5]

Strategic market management actually includes all four management systems: the budgeting system, the projection-based approach of long-range planning, the elements of strategic planning, and the refinements needed to adapt strategic decision making to real time. In strategic market management, a periodic planning process is normally supplemented by techniques that allow the organization to be strategically responsive outside the planning process.[6]

The inclusion of the term market in the phrase "strategic management" emphasizes that strategy development needs to be driven by the market and its environment rather than by an internal orientation. It also points out that the process should be proactive rather than reactive and that the task should be to try to influence the environment as well as respond to it.

Notes

[1] To cope with strategic surprises and fast-developing threats and opportunities, strategic decisions need to be precipitated and made outside the planning cycle.

【译文】为了应对战略上的突然变化以及快速产生的威胁和机遇,我们需要促成计划周期外的战略决策的制定。

【解析】本句中的 surprises 意为"意想不到的事"，在此引申为"突然的变化"。主句是被动形式，翻译时将其转换成主动句比较通顺合理，符合汉语的习惯表达法。
precipitate 意为"促成；使发生"，如：
All this will precipitate an economic crisis.
所有这些将会导致经济危机。

[2] In particular, it suggests a need for continuous, real-time information systems rather than, or in addition to, periodic analysis.

【译文】这种认识尤其表明我们需要的是持续实时的信息系统，而不是或不仅仅是定期分析。

【解析】翻译该句时，首先要根据上下文推导出 it 具体所指什么。在这里，it 指的是上句中的 recognition。另外，翻译时还要注意词性的转换，比如 need 这个词，如果译成名词，那它前面的修饰定语必然太烦冗，而译作动词，则比较通畅平衡。

[3] More sensitive environmental scanning, the identification and continuous monitoring of information-need areas, efforts to develop strategic flexibility and the enhancement of the entrepreneurial thrust of the organization may be helpful.

【译文】我们需要更敏感地审视环境，确认以及不间断地监视需要信息的区域，努力发展战略灵活性，以及提升企业家对机构的推动力，这些都可能是有帮助的。

【解析】翻译这句话的关键是词性的处理，如果单词都按其原先的词性直译过来，那么第一个分句应该是"更加敏感的环境的审视"，不仅生硬，而且意思模糊，译文用"我们"作主语，且将名词转换为动词后原先的问题就轻松解决了。

[4] Rather than simply accepting the environment as given, with the strategic role confined to adaptation and reaction, strategy may be proactive, affecting environmental change.

【译文】战略不是简单地接受给定的环境，也不是扮演适应和回应环境的战略角色，而可能是先发制人的并影响环境变化的。

【解析】本句是由三个伴随状语（Rather than simply accepting the environment as given, with the strategic role confined to adaptation and reaction, affecting environmental change）和一个主句（strategy may be proactive）组成，翻译时理清句子结构就可以了。
proactive 意思是"积极的；有预见的；先发制人的"，根据上文可以知道，原先的战略是被动地接受给定的环境，而现在很可能会采取相反的做法，即主动地去应对或影响环境变化，因此将其译成"先发制人的"，如：
Not reactive, but proactive steps to combat terrorism.
在与恐怖主义的斗争中应先发制人而不能处于被动。

[5] The company is mostly out in front rather than catching up.

【译文】公司应该始终处于领先地位，而不是在追赶他人。

【解析】in front 意为"在前面，在最前面（或最重要）的位置"，这里意译为"处于领先地位"，而 catching up 则译为"追赶他人"，以便与前面的"领先地位"相对应。

[6] In strategic market management, a periodic planning process is normally supplemented by techniques that allow the organization to be strategically responsive outside the planning process.

【译文】在战略市场管理中,定期的规划程序通常要有技术作辅助,这些技术使得机构可以在规划程序外能够保持战略上的灵敏性。

【解析】这句话的定语从句比较长,因此在翻译时通过重复先行词将定语从句后置。关于定语从句的译法,可参见 Unit 2 中的 Translation Skills 一节。

Passage B (English-Chinese Translation)

Brand Loyalty
David A. AAKER

Words & Expressions

Work on the following words and expressions and write the translated version in the space provided:

programs to generate brand loyalty	___
a prime enduring asset	___
installed customer base	___
switching costs	___
a substantial investment	___
enormous sustainable competitive advantages	___
a substantial entry barrier to competitors	___
an established brand	___
the profit potential for the entrant	___
service backup	___
prospective customers	___
give ... some breathing room	___
sensitive indicators of customer satisfaction	___

A customer orientation will lead to a concern for existing customers and programs to generate brand loyalty.[1] A prime enduring asset for some businesses is the loyalty of the installed customer base. Competitors may duplicate or surpass a product or service, but they still face the task of making customers switch brands. Brand loyalty, or resistance to switching, can be based on simple habit (there is no motivation to change from the familiar gas station or supermarket), preference (there is genuine liking of the brand of cake mix or its symbol, perhaps based on use experience over a long time period), or switching costs. Switching costs would be a consideration for a software user, for example, when a substantial investment has already been made in training employees to learn a particular software system.

An existing base of loyal customers provides enormous sustainable competitive advantages. First, it reduces the marketing costs of doing business, since existing customers usually are relatively easy to hold—the familiar is comfortable and reassuring. Keeping existing customers happy and reducing their motivation to change is usually considerably less costly than trying to reach new customers and persuading them to try another brand. Of course, the higher the loyalty, the easier it is to keep customers happy.

Second, the loyalty of existing customers represents a substantial entry barrier to competitors. Significant resources are required when entering a market in which existing customers must be enticed away from an established brand that they are loyal to or even merely satisfied with.[2] The profit potential for the entrant is thus reduced. For the barrier to be effective, however, potential competitors must know about it; they cannot be allowed to entertain the delusion that customers are vulnerable.[3] Therefore, signals of strong customer loyalty, such as advertisements about documented customer loyalty or product quality, can be useful.

Third, relatively large, satisfied customer base provides an image of a brand as an accepted, successful, enduring product that will include service backup and product improvements. For example, Dell computer, a mail-order computer firm, advertised its installed base of loyal customers among the Fortune 500 companies to reassure prospective customers wary of buying a mail-order computer.

Finally, brand loyalty provides the time to respond to competitive moves—it gives a firm some breathing room. If a competitor develops a superior product, a loyal following will allow the firm the time needed to respond by matching or neutralizing.[4] For example, some newly developed high-tech markets have customers who are attracted by the most advanced product of the moment; there is little brand loyalty in this group. In contrast, other markets have loyal, satisfied customers who will not be looking for new products and thus may not learn of an advancement. Furthermore, they will have little incentive to change even if exposed to the new product.[5] With a high level of brand loyalty, a firm can allow itself the luxury of pursuing a less risky follower strategy.[6]

The management of brand loyalty is a key to achieving strategic success. Firms that manage brand loyalty well are likely to

- Place a value on the future purchases expected from a customer so that existing customers receive appropriate resources.
- Measure the loyalty of existing customers. Measurement should include not only sensitive indicators of customer satisfaction but also measures of the relationship between the customer and the brand. Is the brand respected, considered a friend, liked, and trusted?
- Conduct exit interviews with those who leave the brand to locate points of

vulnerability.
- Have a customer culture, whereby people throughout the organization are empowered and motivated to keep the customer happy.
- Reward loyal customers with frequent-buyer programs or special unexpected benefits or premiums.
- Make customers feel that they are part of the organization, perhaps through customer clubs.
- Have continuing communication with customers, using direct mail, the web, toll-free numbers, and a solid customer backup organization.

Notes

[1] A customer orientation will lead to a concern for existing customers and programs to generate brand loyalty.

【译文】以消费者为导向将使我们关注现有的消费者和项目,以发展品牌忠诚。

【解析】lead to 的本义是"导致,通向",但是为了句子的总体连贯性,这里译成"使得"。

[2] Significant resources are required when entering a market in which existing customers must be enticed away from an established brand that they are loyal to or even merely satisfied with.

【译文】当竞争者进入一个新市场的时候,他必须要吸引其中现有的消费者,使得他们从自己所忠诚的或者甚至仅仅是满意的地位稳固的品牌中转移出来,在这个时候,很可能需要花费巨大的资源。

【解析】这个句子中含有多重从句,由 when 引导的时间状语带了一个 which 引导的定语从句,而这个定语从句又带了一个由 that 引导的定语从句,如果直接按照英文语序译出,那句子将显得极其繁复和佶屈聱牙,所以在翻译时对其进行了适当调整,虽然有些不那么紧凑,但毕竟意思明确、文理通顺。

[3] ... they cannot be allowed to entertain the delusion that customers are vulnerable.

【译文】他们不能心存错觉,认为消费者是易受诱惑的。

【解析】entertain 意为"抱有,心存,持有(信心、观点等);招待,接受",本句中取"抱有,持有(信心,观点等)"之意。本句含有一个同位语从句,如把它译成"他们不能心存消费者是易受诱惑的错觉"未尝不可,但读来多少有些别扭。

[4] If a competitor develops a superior product, a loyal following will allow the firm the time needed to respond by matching or neutralizing.

【译文】如果竞争者生产出了更优秀的产品,那么品牌的忠实追随者将会给公司留下一段必需的时间来作出反应,以生产出能与其匹敌或能压制它的产品。

【解析】following 指的是"一批追随者"。needed to respond by matching or neutralizing 是作 time 的后置定语,译成中文的时候注意语序的调整。句中的 neutralize 在这里不宜译成"使中立,使中和",而应该译成"抵制,压制"。

[5] Furthermore, they will have little incentive to change even if exposed to the new product.

【译文】而且,即使他们接触到了新产品,也不会想着去更换。
【解析】这句话结构很简单,翻译的关键在于词义的处理:比如 have little incentive,没必要将其直译为"几乎没有什么动机",把它意译为"不会想"则更加言简意赅;再如 exposed to the new product,意译为"接触到了新产品"即可。

[6] With a high level of brand loyalty, a firm can allow itself the luxury of pursuing a less risky follower strategy.

【译文】高层次的品牌忠诚使得公司可以奉行一个不太冒险的追随者战略,这对于公司本身而言实在是一种奢侈。
【解析】在翻译这句话时,特意将状语 With a high level of brand loyalty 变为主语"高层次的品牌忠诚",保证了句子的整体连贯性。

Passage C （Chinese-English Translation）

自主品牌:市场的直接交锋

创新成功与否,要以市场回报来评价。在国内国际市场竞争中直接交锋的是品牌,接受公众选择的是品牌,最终决定市场竞争胜负的还是品牌。品牌的价值在于企业及其产品的外在性能和内在品质的综合体现,是企业文化力、学习力、创新力,即企业核心竞争力最有说服力的表征。

从另一个角度讲,品牌是企业就其产品和服务,面向市场、面向用户、面向消费者所做出的承诺。具有国际影响力、穿透力、竞争力并成功营销的著名品牌,其品牌信誉和企业诚信可以换来公众对品牌的忠诚,这些著名品牌的价值已从企业扩展到社会,延伸到企业的家园——国家。

随着经济全球化日益深化,跨国公司的全球战略正从产能扩张、技术扩张转向品牌扩张,在对外投资中通过凝聚着巨大无形资产的知名品牌,抢占世界市场财富的优先索取权和分配权。面对严峻的竞争形势,走中国特色自主创新之路,绝不能在科技成果转化、实现科技产业化后就止步不前,必须继续前进,直达创新和营销自主大品牌的目标。

Translation Skills（Ⅳ）

翻译中的词性转换

为了达到最好的表达效果,英语和汉语在表达同一个意思的时候会使用不同的结构来表示,因此为了适应语言的表达习惯和语法规则,我们在翻译中必须运用一些词性和表现方法的转换技巧,而不是一味追求词性和表达方法的对等。在翻译过程中的转换包括词性的转换和句子结构的转换,在本单元我们主要讲解翻译中词性的转换。

在一定程度上,词的形态及形式变化是否过于繁复多变决定了词性优势。英语动词形态变化繁复而稳定,这就使英语动词的使用受形态的掣肘,而名词就没有这个问题,因此名词在英语中占优势,名词的优势导致了介词的伴随优势。汉语词性没有形态变化问题,而动词与名词做比较时,动词的动态感强、动势强,名词则较为凝滞,所以在汉语中动词非常活跃,可连用,也可广泛代替名词。英语倾向于多用名词,因而叙述呈静态(static);汉语倾向于多用动词,因而叙述呈动态(dynamic)。在现代汉语中,一个句子不限于只用一个动词,可以连续使用几个动词,即所谓"动词连用"。动词连用是现代汉语句法的显著特征之一。下面按不同词性的转换分类讲解。

1. 转换为汉语动词

正如我们上面讲解中提到的,汉语倾向于多用动词,因此我们在翻译的过程中,多把英语中的名词(具有动词意义或含有动词意味的名词或有 er,or 后缀的含有强烈动作意味的名词)、形容词(表示心理状态或以 ble 结尾的形容词)、连词或介词(具有动词意义)以及副词译成汉语中的动词。下面我们各举一例来说明:

例1 The thought of future fills me with boundless energy and strength.

译文:一想到将来,我感到浑身有用不完的力气。

例2 He is a regular visitor.

译文:他经常来。

如果例1翻译成"未来的想法让我感到浑身有用不完的力气",按照汉语的理解模式,这种译文自然会产生歧义,也并不是原文所要表达的意思。例2如果翻译为"他是一个有规律的访客",意思传达没错,但不符合汉语的语言习惯。

例3 They were not content with their present achievements.

译文:他们不满足于他们现有的成就。

例4 She is capable of doing so.

译文:她能够这样做。

例5 As long as we have means of producing heat, we can keep the steam engine at work.

译文:只要我们有办法产生热,就能使蒸汽机做功。

例6 The workers are confident that they will be able to build the modern factory in a short time.

译文:工人们确信能在短时期内建成这座现代化的工厂。

2. 名词与副词的互换

英语句子中多用名词,但是在翻译成汉语时,如果依然用名词形式,那整个句子会显得累赘繁杂,甚至难以理解,如:

例7 Perhaps she would prod at the straw in her clumsy impatience.

误译:也许她会以她笨拙地不耐烦去翻弄那个草铺。

译文:也许她会迫不及待地、笨手笨脚地翻弄那个草铺。

显然,从上面举出的误译我们能看出,这样不变词性的翻译是毫无道理的。通常英语句子中意义抽象的名词都会被译为汉语中的副词。要注意的是,当英语名词转换成汉语副词或动词的时候,修饰该名词的形容词要转换为副词。同样,英语句中的副词如果直译为副词,句子会显得很死板。

例8 They have not done so well ideologically, however, as organizationally.

译文:他们的思想工作没有他们的组织工作做得好。

3. 形容词与副词的互换

在上文阐述名词与副词的互换时,我们提到了当英语名词转换成汉语副词或动词的时候,修饰该名词的形容词自然就转换为了副词。反过来,英语动词译成汉语名词的时候,修饰该动词的副词往往转译成形容词。此外,由于英语和汉语的表达方式的不同,有一些形容词是约定俗成地译成了汉语的副词。

例 9 Sometimes we have to pay dearly for mistakes.

译文:有时我们不得不为错误付出高昂的代价。

例 10 We are fortunate to meet you here.

译文:我们很幸运地在这里见到你。

在这一讲中,我们除了理论介绍外,更多地使用了实例来加以阐述。

Translation Exercises

1. To be frank, we find it hard to entertain your claim.
2. Nowadays young people are exposed to much more fierce competition than their forefathers.
3. Brand loyalty reflects the customers' attitude and actions towards the products of companies.
4. The difficulty with the periodic planning process is that the need for strategic analysis and decision making does not always occur on an annual basis.
5. 环境污染会促成很多生物的灭绝。(precipitate)
6. 这种积极、广泛的人际交往对于掌握网络学习方法及对传统课堂教学都有不少有益的启示。(proactive)
7. 这样的军备竞赛只会导致战争。(lead to)
8. 高税收将抵消增加了的工资。(neutralize)

Unit 9

Passage A (English-Chinese Translation)

What Is Consumer Behavior?

Michael R. Solomon

Words & Expressions

Work on the following words and expressions and write the translated version in the space provided:

cover a lot of ground
spiritual fulfillment
role theory
an ongoing process
an integral part of marketing
fashion suicide
a friend's grimace
office supplies
play a pivotal role in doing sth.

    The field of consumer behavior covers a lot of ground: It is the study of the processes involved when individuals or groups select, purchase, use, or dispose of products, services, ideas, or experiences to satisfy needs and desires. Consumers take many forms, ranging from an eight-year-old child begging her mother for Pokemon cards to an executive in a large corporation deciding on a multimillion-dollar computer system. [1] The items that are consumed can include anything from canned peas, a massage, democracy, hip-hop music, or hoopster rebel Dennis Rodman. Needs and desires to be satisfied range from hunger and thirst to love, status, or even spiritual fulfillment. Our attachment to everyday products is exemplified by our love affair with colas. [2] The World Coca-Cola in Las Vegas draws a million visitors a year. Exhibits ask, "What does Coca-Cola mean to you?" and many of the responses tell of strong emotional connections to the brand. [3]

Consumers Are Actors on the Marketplace Stage

The perspective of role theory takes the view that much of consumer behavior resembles actions in a play. As in a play, each consumer has lines, props, and costumes necessary to put on a good performance. Because people act out many different roles, they sometimes alter their consumption decisions depending on the particular "play" they are in at the time. [4] The criteria they use to evaluate products and services in one of their roles may be quite different from those used in another role.

Consumer Behavior Is a Process

In its early stages of development, the field was often referred to as buyer behavior, reflecting an emphasis on the interaction between consumers and producers at the time of purchase. Most markets now recognize that consumer behavior is an ongoing process, not merely what happens at the moment a consumer hands over money or a credit card and in turn receives some good or service.

The exchange, a transaction in which two or more organizations or people give and receive something of value, is an integral part of marketing. Although exchange remains an important part of consumer behavior, the expanded view emphasizes the entire consumption process, which includes the issues that influence the consumer before, during, and after a purchase. [5]

Consumer Behavior Involves Many Different Actors

A consumer is generally thought of as a person who identifies a need or desire, makes a purchase, and then disposes of the product during the three stages in the consumption process. In many cases, however, different people may be involved in this sequence of events. [6] The purchaser and user of a product might not be the same person, as when a parent picks out clothes for a teenager (and makes selection that can result in "fashion suicide" in the view of the teen). In other cases, another person may act as an influencer, providing recommendations for or against certain products without actually buying or using them. For example, a friend's grimace when one tries on a new pair of pants may be more influential than anything a mother or father might do.

Finally, consumers may take the form of organizations or groups. [7] One or several persons may make the decisions involved in purchasing products that will be used by many, as when a purchasing agent orders the company's office supplies. In other organizational situations, purchase decisions may be made by a large group of people—for example, company accountants, designers, engineers, sales personnel, and others—all of whom will have a say in the various stages of the consumption process. One important type of organization is the family, where different family members play pivotal roles in making decisions regarding produces and services used by all.

Notes

[1] Consumers take many forms, ranging from an eight-year-old child begging her mother for Pokemon cards to an executive in a large corporation deciding on a multimillion-dollar computer system.

【译文】消费者包含了多种人,从向母亲乞求口袋怪兽卡片的8岁幼童,到一家大公司中决定价值几百万美元的计算机系统的行政官员。

【解析】Pokemon card 是一种"口袋怪兽卡片游戏"。take many forms 意思是"以多种形式(存在)",文中译为"包含多种人"则比较通顺。此外,原句中的两个定语在翻译时均适合前置,这样才不显拖沓。

[2] Our attachment to everyday products is exemplified by our love affair with colas.

【译文】我们对日常商品的依恋可以以我们与可乐类饮料的情缘为例。

【解析】attachment to ... 意思是"对……的依恋,眷恋,留恋"。此句中的 love affair 不能译为"桃色事件"或"风流韵事",语境不合理,译为"情缘"较合理。

[3] ... many of the responses tell of strong emotional connections to the brand.

【译文】许多的反馈都说起与品牌之间强烈的情感联系。

【解析】tell of 在句中译为"说起"。

[4] Because people act out many different roles, they sometimes alter their consumption decisions depending on the particular "play" they are in at the time.

【译文】因为人们扮演了许多不同的角色,所以他们有时会根据当时所在特定"剧本"来改变他们的消费决定。

【解析】这句话所在的段落是把消费者比作"演员",把市场比作"舞台",因此在翻译这个句子的时候,要联系上下文去理解意思,从而结合语境尽量保持原句的感觉。

[5] Although exchange remains an important part of consumer behavior, the expanded view emphasizes the entire consumption process, which includes the issues that influence the consumer before, during, and after a purchase.

【译文】虽然交易仍然是消费者行为的一个重要组成部分,但其扩展概念则强调了整个消费过程。这一消费过程包含购买前、购买当时以及购买后一切影响消费者的事件。

【解析】该句是典型的非限制性定语从句,因此翻译时采用了后置法,使句子前后平衡的同时,也能达到完整并清楚表达原句意思的目的。

[6] In many cases, however, different people may be involved in this sequence of events.

【译文】然而,在许多情况下,参与这一系列事件的可能不是同一个人。

【解析】这句话的翻译关键是 different people,如果把 different people may be involved in this sequence of events 翻译成"不同的人可能会参与这一系列事件",则不能突出 different 的含义。

[7] Finally, consumers may take the form of organizations or groups.

【译文】最后,消费者也可能会以机构或者团体的形式出现。

【解析】take the form of ... 意为"以……的形式"。

Passage B (English-Chinese Translation)

Core Values
Michael R. Solomon

Words & Expressions

Work on the following words and expressions and write the translated version in the space provided:

subordinate one's identity to the group	_____
virtues of group membership	_____
freedom of expression	_____
reject the conservative behavior of the past	_____
dropout rate	_____
marketing efforts	_____
universal values	_____
reverse pattern	_____
socialization agents	_____
enculturation	_____
acculturation	_____

Every culture has a set of values that it imparts to its members.[1] People in one culture might feel that being a unique individual is preferable to subordinating one's identity to the group, whereas another culture may emphasize the virtues of group membership. A study by Wirthlin Worldwide found that the most important values to Asian executives are hard work, respect for learning, and honesty. In contrast, North American businesspeople emphasize the values of personal freedom, self-reliance, and freedom of expression.

And, of course, a culture's values do change over time—not necessarily in positive ways. Right now in Japan young people are working hard to adopt more Western values and behaviors—which explains why the current fashion for young people is bleached blond hair, chalky makeup, and deep tans. But, as the Japanese are being urged by their government to spend more and to be more free in the way they live, more and more teenagers are starting to reject the conservative behavior of the past. The dropout rate among students in junior and senior high school has increased by 20 percent in a two-year period. More than 50 percent of girls have had intercourse by their senior year, a 10 percent increase since the early 1990s.

These differences in values often explain why marketing efforts that are a big hit in one country can flop in another.[2] For example, a hugely successful advertisement in Japan promoted breast cancer awareness by showing an attractive woman in a sundress drawing stares from men on the street as a voice-over says, "If only women paid as much attention to their breasts as men do." The same ad flopped in France because the use of humor to talk about a serious disease offended the French.

In many cases, of course, values are universal. Who does not desire health, wisdom, or world peace? What sets cultures apart is the relative importance, or ranking, of these universal values. This set of rankings constitutes a culture's value system. For example, one study found that North Americans have more favorable attitudes toward advertising messages that focus on self-reliance, self-improvement, and the achievement of personal goals as opposed to themes stressing family integrity, collective goals, and the feeling of harmony with others.[3] The reverse pattern was found for Korean consumers.

Every culture is characterized by its members' endorsement of a value system.[4] These values may not be equally endorsed by every individual, and in some cases, values may even seem to contradict one another (e. g., Americans appear to value both conformity and individuality, and seek to find some accommodation between the two[5]). Nonetheless, it is usually possible to identify a general set of core values that uniquely define a culture.[6] These beliefs are taught to us by socialization agents, including parents, friends, and teachers. The process of learning the beliefs and behaviors endorsed by one's own culture is termed enculturation. In contrast, the process of learning the value system and behaviors of another culture (often a priority for those who wish to understand consumers and markets in foreign countries) is called acculturation.[7]

Core values such as freedom, youthfulness, achievement, materialism, and activity have been claimed to characterize American culture, but even these basic beliefs are subject to change. For example, Americans' emphasis on youth is eroding as the population ages.

Notes

[1] Every culture has a set of values that it imparts to its members.

【译文】每一种文化都会赋予其成员一整套的价值观。

【解析】这句话中含有定语从句,在翻译时要注意语序的调整。针对这个句子,选用融合法比较合适,也就是将主句与从句融合在一起,利用从句的关系代词与主句某成分的代替关系,根据意思重新组成汉语单句。

[2] These differences in values often explain why marketing efforts that are a big hit in one country can flop in another.

【译文】这些价值观的不同通常解释了为什么在一个国家行之有效的营销手段在另外一个国家却是一败涂地。

【解析】翻译这句话的时候要注意 hit 和 flop 的词性,如果生硬地按原词性翻译,那句子的完整性和连贯性就会受到影响。

[3] For example, one study found that North Americans have more favorable attitudes toward advertising messages that focus on self-reliance, self-improvement, and the achievement of personal goals as opposed to themes stressing family integrity, collective goals, and the feeling of harmony with others.

【译文】比如说,一项研究发现,北美人偏好于在广告中强调自强自立、自我改善和实现个人目标的广告词,而反感于强调家庭整体观念、集体目标以及与他人和谐相处的主题。

【解析】该句篇幅较长,在翻译时要先分析句子结构。显然,句子的大框架是主句(one study found that ...)后跟了一个宾语从句,而这个宾语从句又由另一个主从复合句组成,然后 as opposed to 又引出另外一层意思。翻译时采用了顺译法,使整个句子的意思一目了然。

[4] Every culture is characterized by its members' endorsement of a value system.

【译文】每一种文化都是以其成员对某一价值体系的赞同为特征的。

【解析】be characterized by ... 意思是"以……为特征,……的特点在于……"。

[5] Americans appear to value both conformity and individuality, and seek to find some accommodation between the two.

【译文】美国人好像既重视一致性,又重视个性,而且他们会试图寻找两者之间的融合点。

【解析】该句中 appear to 可以理解为 seem to,也就是"好像,似乎"的意思。conformity 和 individuality 是两个具有相对意义的词,故译为"一致性"与"个性"。

[6] Nonetheless, it is usually possible to identify a general set of core values that uniquely define a culture.

【译文】然而,确定一套普遍的核心价值观来定义一种文化,通常是可能的。

【解析】这是典型的 it 作形式主语的句子。翻译时,为了避免句子结构的不平衡,通常把真正主语提前。

[7] In contrast, the process of learning the value system and behaviors of another culture (often a priority for those who wish to understand consumers and markets in foreign countries) is called acculturation.

【译文】相反,学习另一种文化的价值体系和行为的过程叫作文化适应,这通常是那些想要了解外国消费者和外国市场的商人们优先考虑的。

【解析】原句当中出现了括号,也就是补充说明部分,在翻译时要特别注意处理好句子的结构。译文中把两句融合,既明确表达了意思,又达到了让句子通畅的目的。句中的 acculturation 意为"文化传播,文化的接近、适应和改观",它与 enculturation 的区别在于前者表示去适应他人的文化,而后者则表示适应自己的文化。

Passage C (Chinese-English Translation)

贴牌生产

熟悉加工贸易的人一定对 OEM(original equipment manufacturer)这个词不陌生。

OEM 是指委托生产，俗称"贴牌"。品牌拥有者不直接生产产品，而是利用自己掌握的"核心技术"负责设计和开发新产品，控制销售"渠道"；具体的加工任务交给别的企业去做，承接这项加工任务的制造商就被称为 OEM 厂商，其生产的产品就是 OEM 产品。传统的出口加工区就是 OEM 企业的聚集地，而 OEM 技术在外、资本在外、市场在外、只有生产在内的特征也直接影响了出口加工区的长远发展。

有专家认为，没有品牌就没有定价权，在国际交换中自然处于劣势地位。同时，没有自己的品牌、没有自主创新能力，便没有核心竞争力，就必然受制于人，企业与国家失去的将是可持续发展的动力。

对于企业来讲，品牌建设的重要性毋庸置疑，因为高额的市场占有率和贸易利润谁都不愿错过。但品牌建设非一朝一夕之功，这是一个系统工程，涉及研发、设计、生产、制造、流通、营销等多个环节，是产品性能、质量、效用以及文化和服务的综合体现，需要花费漫长的时间加以孕育。

虽然中国的企业在品牌建设方面任重而道远，但是在贴牌的过程中，我们的企业可以实现资本的原始积累；当进入世界顶级企业的加工生产名单后，企业才会有机会进入主流消费渠道，了解并逐步掌握先进的产品设计与制造理念，才可能在自主品牌的建设道路上走得更远。

Translation Exercises

1. Their economic blandishments take the form of the so-called joint industrial enterprises.
2. Despite their importance, values have not been as widely applied to direct examination of consumer behavior as might be expected.
3. Increases in compulsory contributions range from 30 pence to one pound.
4. Situational factors, such as time pressure or store displays, do affect the consumer's purchase decision.
5. 对于商业欺诈行为应当严厉惩处，而不应姑息养奸。(as opposed to)
6. 他工作的特点是不注意细节。(be characterized by)
7. 这种疾病常表现为持续数天的高烧和呕吐。(take the form of)
8. 这些商品的价格从 500 美元到 5000 美元不等。(range from ... to ...)

Passage A (English-Chinese Translation)

Marketing Strategy

Words & Expressions

Work on the following words and expressions and write the translated version in the space provided:

market saturation	_____
market penetration	_____
consumer product giants	_____
the dominant market share	_____
product life cycle	_____
market niches	_____
product development strategy	_____
existing markets	_____
brand name	_____
brand extension	_____
pollution reduction products	_____
push strategy	_____
distribution system	_____
mass merchandisers	_____
skim pricing	_____
the demand curve	_____

Marketing strategy deals with pricing, selling, and distributing a product. Using a market development strategy, a company or business unit can (1) capture a larger share of an existing market for current products through market saturation and market penetration or (2) develop new markets for current products. Consumer product giants such as Procter & Gamble, Colgate-Palmolive, and Unilever are experts at using advertising and promotion to implement a market saturation/penetration strategy to gain the dominant market share in a product category. As seeming masters of the product life cycle, these companies are able to extend product life almost indefinitely through "new and improved" variations of product and packaging that appeal to most market niches. [1] These companies also follow the second market development strategy by taking a successful product they market in one part of the world and marketing it elsewhere. Noting the success of their presoak detergents in Europe, for example, both P&G and Colgate successfully introduced this type of laundry product to North America under the trade names of Biz and Axion.

Using the product development strategy, a company or unit can (1) develop new products for existing markets or (2) develop new products for new markets. Church & Dwight has had great success following the first product development strategy by developing new products to sell to its current customers. Acknowledging the widespread appeal of its Arm & Hammer brand baking soda, the company generated new uses for its sodium bicarbonate by reformulating it as toothpaste, deodorant, and detergent. [2] Using a successful brand name to market other products is called brand extension and is a good way to appeal to a company's current customers. Sara Lee Corporation (famous for its frozen cheesecake) is taking the same approach by putting the Sara Lee name on various new food products, such as premium meats and fresh baked goods. Arm & Hammer successfully followed the second product development strategy by developing new pollution reduction products (using sodium bicarbonate compounds) for sale to coal-fired electric utility plants—a very different market from grocery stores.

There are numerous other marketing strategies. For advertising and promotion, for example, a company or business unit can choose between a "push" or a "pull" marketing strategy. [3] Many large food and consumer products companies in the United States and Canada have followed a push strategy by spending a large amount of money on trade promotion in order to gain or hold shelf space in retail outlets. Trade promotion includes discounts, in-store special offers, and advertising allowances designed to "push" products through the distribution system. The Kellogg Company recently decided to change its emphasis from a push to a pull strategy, in which advertising "pulls" the products through the distribution channels. [4] The company now spends more money on consumer advertising designed to build brand awareness so that shoppers will ask for the products. Research has indicated that a high level of advertising (a key part of a pull strategy) is most beneficial to leading brands in a market.

Other marketing strategies deal with distribution and pricing. Should a company use distributors and dealers to sell its products or should it sell directly to mass merchandisers? Using both channels simultaneously can lead to problems. In order to increase the sales of its lawn tractors and mowers, for example, John Deere decided to sell the products not only through its current dealer network, but also through mass merchandisers like Home Depot. Deere's dealers, however, were furious. They considered Home Depot to be a key competitor. The dealers were concerned that Home Depot's ability to underprice them would eventually lead to their becoming little more than repair facilities for their competition and left with insufficient sales to stay in business.[5]

When pricing a new product, a company or business unit can follow 1 of 2 strategies. For new-product pioneers, skim pricing offers the opportunity to "skim the cream" from the top of the demand curve with a high price while the product is novel and competitors are few. Penetration pricing, in contrast, attempts to hasten market development and offers the pioneer the opportunity to use the experience curve to gain market share with a low price and dominate the industry. Depending on corporate and business unit objectives and strategies, either of these choices may be desirable to a particular company or unit.[6] Penetration pricing is, however, more likely than skim pricing to raise a unit's operating profit in the long term.

Notes

[1] As seeming masters of the product life cycle, these companies are able to extend product life almost indefinitely through "new and improved" variations of product and packaging that appeal to most market niches.

【译文】这些公司表面上作为产品寿命周期的控制者,几乎可以无止境地通过创新和改良产品种类和包装来吸引小众市场从而延长产品寿命。

【解析】product life cycle 指"产品寿命周期";seeming masters 若直译成"表面上的主人"会显得比较拗口,所以译作"控制者"使表达更加贴切。

appeal to 意思是"引起兴趣,对……有吸引力"。

market niches 又称为 niche markets,汉语里译作"小众市场",是相对于"大众市场"的概念而言的。

[2] Acknowledging the widespread appeal of its Arm & Hammer brand baking soda, the company generated new uses for its sodium bicarbonate by reformulating it as toothpaste, deodorant, and detergent.

【译文】认识到 Arm & Hammer 牌小苏打对客户具有普遍的吸引力,公司于是将小苏打重新配制成牙膏、除臭剂和清洁剂使其产生新的用途。

【解析】这里的 appeal 作名词,意思是"吸引力"。

baking soda = sodium bicarbonate,意为"小苏打,碳酸氢钠"。

reformulating 由 formulate 加前缀而来,formulate 指"配置,制定……的配方",相应的名词形式是 formula。

[3] For advertising and promotion, for example, a company or business unit can choose between a "push" or a "pull" marketing strategy.

【译文】比如说,一家公司或是商务单位为了做广告和促销,会在后推战略和前拉战略二者中选择其一作为其营销策略。

【解析】本句中 promotion 表示"(商品的)宣传,推销,促销"等意思,此外还可以表示"提升,晋升"。

push strategy(后推战略)指制造商通过某种销售渠道推销商品的一种方法,在这种情况下制造商通过商业折扣、广告津贴等营销活动集中在分销商身上,其目的是获得高水平的可供率,希望销售额会随之而来。pull strategy(前拉战略)指制造商通过某种销售渠道推销商品的一种方法,在这种情况下制造商把营销活动瞄准最终消费者,从而创造出对商品的需求,这一需求对商品通过销售系统的销售有前拉作用。

[4] The Kellogg Company recently decided to change its emphasis from a push to a pull strategy, in which advertising "pulls" the products through the distribution channels.

【译文】凯乐格公司最近决定将其营销策略的重点从后推战略转向前拉战略,即通过销售渠道以广告拉动产品销售。

【解析】凯乐格公司是一家从事食品生意、在国内市场居领先地位的跨国公司,主营饼干、糕点等休闲食品。

[5] The dealers were concerned that Home Depot's ability to underprice them would eventually lead to their becoming little more than repair facilities for their competition and left with insufficient sales to stay in business.

【译文】经销商认为家得宝有能力将商品以低于他们的价格出售,这最终会使他们沦为家得宝的维修商店,同时使他们没有足够的销售额来继续从事该行业。

【解析】Home Depot 中文名为"家得宝公司",这是一家成立于1978年的美国公司,是全球最大的家庭装潢专业零售商,也是美国第二大零售商。
becoming little more than repair facilities 字面意思是"跟修理设施没什么两样",这里译为"沦为家得宝的维修商店"。这个说法目的是要表达出与家得宝公司相比,经销商的地位微乎其微,而且由于家得宝的挤压,经销商的销售额会下降,客户会减少,直至被挤出该行业。但是经销商又不能是"维修设施",所以将 repair facilities 译作"维修商店",符合上下文的语境。

[6] Depending on corporate and business unit objectives and strategies, either of these choices may be desirable to a particular company or unit.

【译文】根据公司或商务单位的目标和策略,任一选择都可能适用于特定的公司或单位。

Passage B (English-Chinese Translation)

Managing Innovation
John Storey

Words & Expressions

Work on the following words and expressions and write the translated version in the space provided:

knowledge economy　　　　　　　　　　　_____

Department of Trade and Industry　　　　　_____

sustained behaviour in practice　　　　　　_____

issues of financing and short-termism
the successful exploitation of new ideas
high on the agenda
despite the wealth of concern and activity
innovation research
managerial behaviour
critical participants
general consensus
surface explanations

John Storey reports the results of a three-year research project exploring how managers understand and prioritize innovation and the ways they interpret the factors promoting or inhibiting innovation in their organizations.

The importance of innovation is widely proclaimed. The message has been pressed in varying degrees for over a century, but it has perhaps rarely been argued so insistently as now, in the context of the "knowledge economy". [1] Yet in comparison with the rhetoric, actual performance on this front appears deficient—especially in the UK, where the DTI's (Department of Trade and Industry) innovation/R&D index reveals poor participation by firms. Organizations are more than happy to use the concept of innovation in their advertising and corporate PR, but, apart from a few notable exceptions, sustained behaviour in practice seems below par. [2]

This gap between proclamation and practice requires some explanation. The "problem" of innovation is itself of long standing. The barriers to innovation have been investigated at many levels and from diverse perspectives. For example, issues of financing and short-termism have been highlighted at the macro level, while others have focused on organizational structures and cultures.

Innovation involves much more than invention. The Department of Trade and Industry in the UK has defined it as "the successful exploitation of new ideas". Such an activity requires a whole series of management processes: environmental scanning, an understanding of threats and opportunities, an assessment of internal capabilities, the acquisition and mobilization of resources and capabilities, and the deployment and management of those resources and capabilities in pursuit of the chose end. [3] In sum, innovation is, in essence, a management process.

The subject of innovation is currently high on the agenda of policy makers and managers. The theme has, however, a long and enduring legacy, and the body of literature and research on the subject is extensive. [4] Despite the wealth of concern and activity, the impact of innovation research on actual managerial behaviour appears to be limited.

Innovation ultimately derives from managerial perceptions of the need for the change, the perception of the opportunity to change, and the perceptions about the way to change.[5] Perceptions, beliefs, and assumptions are thus vital aspects to be understood.

In a major three-year research project, a team from the UK's Open University Business School set out to examine the issue of innovation by viewing it through the eyes of some of the most critical participants in the process—i. e., managers, the people who establish priorities, devise strategies, allocate resources, control rewards, and manage performance. The team interviewed nearly 350 managers in over 20 organizations in order to explore how they understand and prioritize innovation and the way they interpret the factors that promote or inhibit innovation in their organizations. A large range of sectors was covered, including pharmaceuticals, computers, banking and finance, television, telecommunications, and call centers, as well as voluntary sector organizations such as Oxfam.

The research found that in most organizations, there is no general consensus among managers about the place or importance of innovation. Even among top team members, there is typically significant variation in judgement about the wisdom of pursuing an innovative, fast follower, or some other strategy.[6]

While an organization may house very creative and inventive individuals, it can be poor at translating novel ideas into products and services with a market impact. The managers in our research produced a wealth of explanations for this phenomenon, including lack of resources (time and money); short-termism; people confined to (and indeed sometimes preferring) their narrow "boxes"; and fear of failure, as it was safer to follow the routine than take risks. These were the surface explanations, but we were able to reveal problems at a deeper level.

Notes

[1] The message has been pressed in varying degrees for over a century, but it has perhaps rarely been argued so insistently as now, in the context of the "knowledge economy".

【译文】一个多世纪以来,这一观点被不同程度地倡导过,但是像现在这样在知识经济的大背景下被反复讨论实属罕见。

【解析】the message 是指文中第一句提到的"创新的重要性",这里译作"观点"比"信息"更贴切。

knowledge economy 意为"知识经济"。

[2] Organizations are more than happy to use the concept of innovation in their advertising and corporate PR, but, apart from a few notable exceptions, sustained behaviour in practice seems below par.

【译文】 一些机构非常喜欢在广告和企业公关中使用"创新"这个概念,但是,除了一些特例外,持续的实践行为远没有达到创新的要求。

【解析】 PR 是 public relations 的缩写。

par 指"一般水平或标准",below par 是"在标准以下"的意思,本句中是"在创新的标准以下"的意思,所以这里翻译成"达不到创新的要求"。par 在商务英语里还等同于 par value,即"(证券与股票的)票面价值"的意思。

sustained 意为"持续不变的",如 sustained growth(持续增长),sustained development(可持续发展)。

[3] Such an activity requires a whole series of management processes: environmental scanning, an understanding of threats and opportunities, an assessment of internal capabilities, the acquisition and mobilization of resources and capabilities, and the deployment and management of those resources and capabilities in pursuit of the chose end.

【译文】 这一活动要求施行一系列的管理过程,如环境扫描、对威胁和机遇的认知、对内部能力的评估、资源和能力的获得与动员以及在追求既定目标过程中对这些资源和能力的调动和管理。

【解析】 chose 在这里用作 choose 的过去分词,这种用法在当代英语中已经废弃,现常用 chosen 作为 choose 的过去分词。in pursuit of the chose end 意为"追求既定目标"。

[4] The theme has, however, a long and enduring legacy, and the body of literature and research on the subject is extensive.

【译文】 创新这一主题由来已久,关于这个主题的文献和研究内容也相当广泛。

【解析】 a long and enduring legacy 直译的意思是"一项长久的遗产",但如果与"创新这一主题"连用,就显得别扭,所以将其意译为"由来已久",这样与创新这一主题连用,就合乎逻辑了。

the body of literature and research on the subject 字面意思是"关于这个主题的文献和研究的主体",但是如果直译的话,会出现"主体很广泛"这样的表达,同样显得别扭,因此这里把它译作"内容相当广泛",符合汉语的表达习惯。

[5] Innovation ultimately derives from managerial perceptions of the need for the change, the perception of the opportunity to change, and the perceptions about the way to change.

【译文】 创新最终来源于三个方面,一是对转变这一需求的管理洞察力,二是对可以带来转变的机遇的洞察力,三是对转变方式的洞察力。

【解析】 该句的译文中增译了"三个方面"以及"一是""二是"和"三是",目的是使句子结构更清晰,让读者对句意一目了然。

derive from 意思是"取得;来自",如:

The original capital of a corporation is usually derived from the sale of capital stock.

公司的初始资本通常来源于资本股的出售。

[6] Even among top team members, there is typically significant variation in judgement about the wisdom of pursuing an innovative, fast follower, or some other strategy.

【译文】即使在顶尖团队成员中,对追随一个敏锐且具有创新能力的人或者追求其他别的战略的判断,也存在着典型不同的看法。

【解析】wisdom 通常作"智慧"解,这里的意思是"看法,意见",如 accepted wisdom(公认的看法)。

Passage C (Chinese-English Translation)

中西方管理模式的不同

西方管理模式和中国管理模式的最大差别就在于"可重复性"。事实上,现代企业管理之所以取得如此辉煌的成就,正是基于每一个岗位或职务的"可重复性"而得以实现的,或者说,正是岗位或职务"可重复性/可替换性"的出现,才使得企业成就、成果的出现成为可能,但并不仅仅依赖于任何一个拥有个人才能的人。但是,在中国管理模式中,没有人会将"老板"看作是一个岗位或职务,通常来说,人们看见的是一个有血有肉、充满商业智慧和人格魅力的人,他的企业只属于他自己,因为他卓越的商业才华是不可重复的,这正是中国商业或企业"富不过三代"的本质原因。更确切地说,中国传统商业的管理逻辑认知是发生在"人"的层面,而并不是"组织"层面。它所强调的是个人的悟性,而不是建设组织能力。这也正是中国可以诞生出伟大的商人,却总是难以造就出一个伟大的商业组织的根本原因。

Translation Skills (V)

长句的翻译

英语长句的翻译一向是翻译中的一大难点,而在商务英语中长句的出现频率很高,因为商务英语问题多为论述性、解释性的。造成翻译长句困难的直接原因是英语和汉语语序的差异和表达的差异。英语句子结构紧凑严密,句中主干结构突出,抽象名词和介词用得较多。英语在表达较复杂的思想时,往往开门见山,然后借助英语特有词汇关系代词进行空间搭架,把各个从句有机地结合起来,因此构成的句子恰似一串葡萄,主干可能很短,上面却结着累累果实。而汉语句子简练明快,动词用得较多,在表达一些较复杂的思想时,往往借助于动词,按时间顺序、逻辑顺序,逐点交代,层层铺开,给人以舒缓明快的感觉。其句子结构好比一根竹竿,一节一节连下去。从总体来看,英语长句比汉语长句多得多。因此我们的讲解以英语长句的汉译为主。

我们在翻译长句的时候,最重要的是要紧缩主干。首先通读全句,根据主谓结构等确定句子的种类,是简单句、并列句还是复合句;进而找出句中的主要成分,即主语和谓语;然后再分清句子中的宾语、状语、定语等成分。与此同时,识别清楚谓语的形态、时态、语气等。表达的时候特别要注意不拘泥于原文的形式,要按照汉语的特点和表达习惯重新加以组合,摆脱英语原文结构上的限制,同时要考虑原文的文体特征,以最终确切地表达原意。总之,我们翻译的目的不是再现原文的语法形式,而是传达原文的思想内容。

下面我们就英语长句的翻译总结了几种翻译技巧:

1. 化整为零法(分切法)

所谓化整为零法就是指在翻译英语长句时,根据英汉两种语言特点,采用拆句、断句、分割、省略、词性转换等手段将英语长句化整为零,译成符合汉语表达习惯的若干汉语短句,便于读者理解,达到通顺易懂的要求。具体地说,就是在原句中的关系代词、主谓连接、并列或转折连接、后续成分与其主体的连接等处,按照意群切断,译成汉语的分句。化整为零法是最常用、最便利也是最有效的长句汉译法。

例1　The President said at a press conference dominated by questions on yesterday's election results that he could not explain why the Republicans had suffered such a widespread defeat, which in the end would deprive the Republican Party of long-held superiority in the House.

译文:在一次记者招待会上,问题集中于昨天的选举结果,总统就此发了言。他说他不能够解释为什么共和党遭到了这样大的失败。这种情况最终会使共和党失去在众院中长期享有的优势。

这一句话当中有着定语后置、宾语从句、定语从句等多种形式的英语语法现象,我们在翻译的时候采用了化整为零的方法,译成了三个单句。

2. 顺译法(顺序法)

顺译法也就是顺水推舟的意思。这种方法仅适用于英语长句和汉语长句的表达方式基本一致的情况,在对这种长句的翻译过程中,译文的语序和英语长句的语序基本保持一致。

例2　But now it is realized that supplies of some of them are limited, and it is even possible to give a reasonable estimate of their "expectation of life", the time it will take to exhaust all known sources and reserves of these materials.

译文:可是现在人们意识到,其中有些矿物质的蕴藏量是有限的,人们甚至还可以比较合理地估计出这些矿物质"可望存在多少年",也就是说,经过若干年后,这些矿物的全部已知矿源和储量将消耗殆尽。

该句的骨干结构为 It is realized that ...,其中 it 为形式主语,that 引导着主语从句以及并列的 it is even possible to ... 结构,其中不定式作主语,the time ... 是 expectation of life 的同位语,进一步解释其含义,而 time 后面的句子是它的定语从句。五个谓语结构表达了四个层次的意义:A. 可是现在人们意识到;B. 其中有些矿物质的蕴藏量是有限的;C. 人们甚至还可以比较合理地估计出这些矿物质"可望存在多少年";D. 将这些已知矿源和储量消耗殆尽的时间。根据同位语从句的翻译方法,我们需要把第四层意义的表达作适当的调整,从而得到以上译文。

3. 倒译法(逆序法)

英语中有些长句的表达次序与汉语表达习惯不同,甚至完全相反,这时就必须从原文后译起,采用倒译法。

例3　We are weary of the danger of colonialism, the division it has brought to our continent, the bloodshed and confusion, the racism and hate that go hand in glove with the colonists.

译文：殖民主义的威胁，殖民主义给我们大陆造成的分裂、流血和混乱，以及与殖民主义者结有不解之缘的种族主义和种族仇恨，这一切我们都受够了。

这句话是将原文的主语放在最后译出，这样的表达清晰明了、一目了然。其实常用的倒译法是将英语长句的句首或某一部分在汉译时置于全句之尾，这种译法多用于主句部分主谓成分较简洁的情况。

4. 插入法(符号法)

所谓插入法就是利用冒号、括号、破折号等标点符号将难以处理的句子成分插入到句中，这样会使得插入成分显而易见，同时译文又通顺明了。

例4 When I went to Yan'an in summer of 1946, the Anti-Japanese War, and the Second World War of which it was a part, had been over for just a year.

译文：我在1946年夏天去延安的时候，抗日战争和第二次世界大战（抗日战争是第二次世界大战的组成部分）结束了刚刚1年。

我们以上只介绍了几种常用的翻译长句的方法，此外还有重组法、包孕法、拆句法等，这些方法从字面上看就可以理解，我们不再做精讲。其实各种翻译方法之间并不是完全分离的，因为英语长句情况十分复杂，有时要翻译好一个长句只用一种方法是解决不了问题的，这时候我们就需要熟练地综合利用以上各种翻译方法。

Translation Exercises

1. They are interested in foreign trade or investment because of the direct and indirect profits derived from it.
2. Several doctors are researching on a formula for a new drug.
3. The total par value of all issued stock constitutes the legal capital of the corporation.
4. He believes sustained economic growth will provide a sound economic foundation for further development of the insurance sector.
5. 请务必使包装对年轻人有吸引力。(appeal to)
6. 做广告往往是最好的推销方法。(promotion)
7. 不能以污染环境为代价来寻求工业的发展。(pursue)
8. 管理部门在广泛听取意见和仔细研究之后做出了这一决定。(extensive)

Passage A (English-Chinese Translation)

The Manager, the Organization, and the Team
Samuel J. Mantel Jr.

Words & Expressions

| Work on the following words and expressions and write the translated version in the space provided: |

senior management _____
project manager _____
prospective PM _____
talents and knowledge _____
be apt to ... _____
a carefully coordinated set of activities _____
be functionally organized _____
well-defined components or technologies _____
an arm's-length client _____
project budgets _____
project management software _____
resource allocation _____
the meat of the PM's job _____
stubborn functional managers and clients _____

Once a project has been selected, the next step is for senior management to choose a project manager (PM). It is the PM's job to make sure that the project is properly planned, implemented, and completed.

While PMs are sometimes chosen prior to a project's selection, the more typical case is that the selection is announced following a meeting between senior management and the prospective PM. This appointment sometimes comes as a complete surprise to the candidate whose only obvious qualification for the job is not being otherwise fully occupied on a task more important than the project. [1] At this meeting, the senior manager describes the project and emphasizes its importance to the parent organization, and also to the future career of the prospective PM. (In the language of the Mafia, "It's an offer you can't refuse.")[2]

After a brief consideration of the project, the PM comes to a tentative decision about what talents and knowledge are apt to be required.[3] The PM then calls a meeting of people who have the requisite talent and knowledge, and the planning begins. First, we must examine the skills required by the person who will lead a team of individuals to carry out a carefully coordinated set of activities in an organizational setting seemingly designed expressly to prevent cooperation.[4] It is helpful if we make a few mild assumptions to ease the following discussions. First, assume that the project's parent organization is medium- to large-size, and is functionally organized (i.e., organized into functions such as marketing, manufacturing, R&D, human resources, and the like). Further assume that the project has some well-defined components or technologies and that the project's output is being delivered to an arm's-length client.[5] These assumptions are not critical. They merely give a context to our discussions.

Before we proceed, an experienced project manager has suggested that we share with the reader one of her reactions to the materials in this book. To the student or the inexperienced PM, it is the project budgets, the schedules with Gantt charts and PERT/CPM networks, the reports and project management software, and the mysteries of resource allocation to multiple projects that appear to be the meat of the PM's job. But these things are not hard to learn, and once understood can, for the most part, be managed by making appropriate inputs to project management software. The hard part of project management is playing the many roles of the PM.[6] The hard part is negotiating with stubborn functional managers and clients who have their own legitimate axes to grind.[7] The hard part is keeping the peace among project team members each of whom know, and are quick to tell, the proper ways to do things. The hard part is being surrounded by the chaos of trying to run a project in the midst of a confused mass of activity representing the normal business of the organization.[8]

Notes

[1]　This appointment sometimes comes as a complete surprise to the candidate whose only obvious qualification for the job is not being otherwise fully occupied on a task more important than the project.

【译文】这一任命有时完全出于候选人意料之外,因为该候选人唯一显而易见的资质只是目前他并不在参与一项比此项目更为重要的工作。

【解析】appointment 这里不是指"约会",而是"任命,委任"的意思。

qualification 意为"资格,资质",如 qualification certificate(资格证书)。

not being otherwise fully occupied on a task 意为"并非另有任务"。

[2] In the language of the Mafia, "It's an offer you can't refuse."

【译文】用黑手党的话来说,"这是个不容拒绝的好差使。"

【解析】Mafia(黑手党):意大利西西里的一个秘密恐怖组织,被指控为跨国界的犯罪组织,自19世纪以来在意大利和美国特别活跃。in the language of the Mafia 意为"用黑手党的话来说",含有不容违拗的语气。这里用来喻指 senior manager 的口吻非常强硬,是命令式的,完全不容争辩。

offer 这里是"建议,提议"的意思,商务英语里经常表示"报价,发盘",如:

We are working on your offer of 2,000 kilos black tea.

我们正在处理你方 2000 公斤茶叶的报盘。

[3] ... the PM comes to a tentative decision about what talents and knowledge are apt to be required.

【译文】……项目经理对该项目可能要求的才干和知识做出试探性的决定。

【解析】tentative 意为"试探性的,尝试性的",如 tentative purchase(试购)。

be apt to 意为"易于,倾向于",根据句意这里译作"可能"。

[4] First, we must examine the skills required by the person who will lead a team of individuals to carry out a carefully coordinated set of activities in an organizational setting seemingly designed expressly to prevent cooperation.

【译文】首先,我们必须检验一下这个人所需的技能,此人将领导一个由许多个体组成的团队,在一个表面上明显是为了防止合作而设定的组织环境中去完成一组精心协调好的活动。

【解析】原句成分较复杂,句子太长,翻译时做了适当的断句处理。

[5] Further assume that the project has some well-defined components or technologies and that the project's output is being delivered to an arm's-length client.

【译文】再进一步假设项目的各个组成部分和各项技术都很明确,项目的产出正被交付给近在咫尺的客户。

【解析】短语 at arm's length 表示"以一臂之远;在伸手可及处",所以这里将 an arm's-length client 译作"近在咫尺的客户"。

[6] The hard part of project management is playing the many roles of the PM.

【译文】项目管理难就难在扮演好项目经理的多种角色。

[7] The hard part is negotiating with stubborn functional managers and clients who have their own legitimate axes to grind.

【译文】项目管理难就难在与固执的职能部门经理以及客户进行磋商,因为这些人都有私心。

【解析】have an axe to grind 意思是"有私心,别有企图"。

functional managers 指"职能部门经理"。公司里的采购部(purchasing department)、人力资源部(HR department)、会计部(accounting department)以及营销部(marketing department)等都属于职能部门。动词 function 意为"行使职能",如:

In a small company, the bookkeeper may also function as a cashier, or as an

assistant to the manager.
在一家小公司里,簿记员也可能兼任出纳或经理助理等职。

[8] The hard part is being surrounded by the chaos of trying to run a project in the midst of a confused mass of activity representing the normal business of the organization.

【译文】项目管理难就难在在令人心烦意乱的一大堆公司常规商务活动中管理该项目。

【解析】本文最后一段以四个排比句结尾,所以汉译时也应该保留排比句格式,四个 The hard part 均译为"项目管理难就难在……",这样就显得比较工整。

句中 be surrounded by the chaos 和 in the midst of a confused mass 其实要表达的都是一个意思,所以翻译时可以省去前面部分,使表达更加简洁。

Passage B (English-Chinese Translation)

Leadership, Style, Ethics
Samuel J. Mantel Jr.

Words & Expressions

Work on the following words and expressions and write the translated version in the space provided:

be decomposed into ...
the best managerial style
technological uncertainty
a strong sense of ethics
all parties-at-interest
kickback
bribery
use of substandard materials
high administrative and technical credibility
sensitivity to interpersonal conflict

A leader is someone who indicates to other individuals or groups the direction in which they should proceed. [1] When complex projects are decomposed into a set of tasks and subtasks, it is common for members of the project to focus on their individual tasks, thereby ignoring the project as a whole. This fosters the dreaded suboptimization that we mentioned earlier. Only the PM is in a position to keep team members working toward completion of the whole project rather than its parts. In practice, leaders keep their people energized, enthusiastic, well organized, and well informed. [2] This, in turn, will keep the team well motivated.

Previously, we noted that the PM's role should be facilitative rather than authoritarian. Now let us consider the style with which that role is played. There has been much research on the best managerial style for general management, and it has been assumed that the findings apply to PMs as well. Recent work has raised some questions about this assumption. While there is little doubt that the most effective overall style is participative, Professor Shenhar of the Stevens Institute of Technology adds another dimension to style.[3] He found that as the level of technological uncertainty of a project went from "low tech" to "very high tech", the appropriate management style (while being fundamentally participative) went from "firm" to "highly flexible". In addition, he found that the complexity of the project, ranked from "simple" to "highly complex", called for styles varying from "informal" to "highly formal".[4] To sum up, the more technically uncertain a project, the more flexible the style of management should be. The more complex a project, the more formal the style should be. In this context, flexibility applies primarily to the degree that new ideas and approaches are considered. Formality applies primarily to the degree to which the project operates in a structured environment.[5]

Professor Shenhar's work has the feeling of good sense. When faced with technological uncertainty, the PM must be open to experimentation.[6] In the same way, if a project is highly complex with many parts that must be combined with great care, the PM cannot allow a haphazard approach by the project team. In the end, the one reasonably sure conclusion about an effective management style for PMs is that it must be participative. Autocrats do not make good project managers.

Another aspect of leadership is for the PM to have—and to communicate—a strong sense of ethics. Because projects differ from one to another, there are few standard procedures that can be installed to ensure honest and ethical behavior from all parties-at-interest to the project. One has only to read a daily paper to find examples of kickbacks, bribery, covering up mistakes, use of substandard materials, theft, fraud, and outright lies on project status or performance. Dishonesty on anyone's part should not be permitted in projects.

Successful PMs have some common characteristics. They are "closers". They also have high administrative and technical credibility, show sensitivity to interpersonal conflict, and possess the political know-how to get help from senior management when needed. In addition, the PM should be a leader, and adopt a participatory management style that may have to be modified depending on the level of technological sophistication and uncertainty involved in the project.[7] Another critical project management skill is the ability to direct the project in an ethical manner.

Notes

[1]   A leader is someone who indicates to other individuals or groups the direction in

which they should proceed.
领导者是为其他个人或团体指引前进方向的人。

【译文】proceed 这里作动词,意为"继续前进,继续进行",在商务英语中,作名词的 proceeds 表示"(从事某种活动或变卖财物等的)收入,收益",如:

【解析】They gave a concert and donated the proceeds to charity.
他们举办了一次音乐会,把收入捐给了慈善机构。

[2] In practice, leaders keep their people energized, enthusiastic, well organized, and well informed.

【译文】在实际工作中,领导者要使他的属下始终保持精力旺盛、热情洋溢、有条不紊和见多识广。

【解析】这个句子虽然理解起来比较容易,但是翻译起来并不那么简单,译文用四字格式将原句结尾的四个形容词译出,不仅内容上符合原意,形式上也工整对仗。

[3] While there is little doubt that the most effective overall style is participative, Professor Shenhar of the Stevens Institute of Technology adds another dimension to style.

【译文】虽然普遍认为参与式的管理风格是最有效、最全面的,但史蒂文斯科技学院的 Shenhar 教授还是对这种管理风格增加了一个方面。

【解析】这里 dimension 意为"特点;方面",如:
The new findings have added another dimension to man's early story.
这些新发现为人类早期历史又增加了一个方面。

[4] In addition, he found that the complexity of the project, ranked from "simple" to "highly complex", called for styles varying from "informal" to "highly formal".

【译文】此外,他发现随着项目的复杂性由低到高,管理风格也要随之由非正式转为高度正式。

【解析】虽然原句中将复杂性按 simple 到 highly complex 排列,汉语中我们习惯用"由低到高"来形容事情的复杂程度,所以这里没有直译成"由简单到高度复杂",而意译成了"由低到高"。

[5] In this context, flexibility applies primarily to the degree that new ideas and approaches are considered. Formality applies primarily to the degree to which the project operates in a structured environment.

【译文】这就意味着,有新的意见和方法产生时,灵活的管理风格比较适用,而当项目的运行是在一个组织严密的环境里进行时,正式的管理风格更加适用。

【解析】in this context 直译应该是"在这个背景下",这里可以意译为"这就是说,这就意味着"。

flexibility 和 formality 根据上下文的意思,具体增译为"灵活的管理风格"和"正式的管理风格"。

[6] When faced with technological uncertainty, the PM must be open to experimentation.

【译文】项目经理在遇到技术不确定的麻烦时,应该欢迎用实验来解决问题。

【解析】句中be open to原意是"对……开放",如果直译成"项目经理必须对实验开放",意思表达不明确,所以译文先将从句中faced with technological uncertainty译成"遇到技术不确定的麻烦",通过增译"麻烦"一词,引出后面"欢迎用实验来解决问题(即麻烦)"。

[7] In addition, the PM should be a leader, and adopt a participatory management style that may have to be modified depending on the level of technological sophistication and uncertainty involved in the project.

【译文】此外,项目经理必须是一个采用参与式管理风格的领导者,能随时根据项目所包含的技术的复杂程度和不确定性改进自己的管理。

【解析】参考译文将这个句子中的be a leader和adopt a participatory management style两个并列成分合在一起,使后者作前者的定语,从而使汉语译文显得更加简洁。sophistication这里指"(技术的)复杂性"。

Passage C (Chinese-English Translation)

经济全球化对企业人才管理的挑战

信息技术和互联网的发展,加快了经济全球化的步伐,打破了国与国之间、地区与地区之间的界限,带来了资本、商品和技术在国际范围内的流动和合理配置,各国贸易、金融、服务等越来越紧密地联系在一起,国际合作和国际化经营十分普遍,地区经济甚至全球经济牵一发而动全身,正日益成为一个不可分割的整体。

经济全球化的表现之一就是生产经营的跨国化。国家之间的关系已经不再局限于最终产品的交换关系,而是越来越多地转变为由跨国公司所组织的产品及其零部件直至工艺的分工关系。当前,跨国公司的生产经营在全球经济中的比重越来越大,在跨国公司的全球战略部署下,产品及其零部件的生产经营主要取决于各种生产要素的优化配置,而国家的差别正在日益淡化。一方面,跨国公司要面对不同国家的政治体制、法律法规和风俗习惯,同时又要推动各种文化的相互了解和不断融合;管理者既要面对来自不同国家、具有不同文化背景和语言的人才,组织他们共同完成任务,又要进行相互沟通、相互协调。另一方面,对企业人力资源的素质也提出了更高的要求,要求人力资源掌握先进的技能,能够独当一面,有较强的可溶性和可塑性,能够不断学习、不断创新,将知识转化为直接生产力。

所以经济全球化对现代企业人才管理提出了新的挑战,要求企业拥有具有战略性、开放性、前瞻性的人才;要求创新企业人才管理的思路和方法。只有掌握现代创新能力的人才,才能成为生产力中最活跃的因素;只有培养和吸纳有创新能力的人才,才能实现企业的可持续发展。

Translation Exercises

1. We will remit you the commission as soon as we have collected the proceeds from the L/C.
2. However, expertise is likely to develop rapidly. And in some countries there is

already considerable sophistication.
3. If you ask a manager what he does, he will most likely tell you that he plans, organizes, coordinates, and controls.
4. We have no wish to sell, but if you make a fair offer, it shall have attention.
5. 董事会全票通过对于一位公共关系官员的任命。(appointment)
6. 他在许多方面有资格担当这项任务。(qualification)
7. 目前我方工厂正忙于交付已订之货。(occupy)
8. 他是一个在政治上并无个人打算的人。(have an axe to grind)

Passage A (English-Chinese Translation)

Industrial Park Leads Suzhou's Eastward Development
Li Jian

Words & Expressions

Work on the following words and expressions and write the translated version in the space provided:

management committee of Suzhou Industrial Park	_____
Yangtze River Delta region	_____
central business district	_____
shopping malls	_____
high-tech research capabilities	_____
global manufacturing base	_____
alleviate pressure	_____
historic relics preservation	_____
real estate developers	_____

Area's future lies in high-tech research capabilities, innovations and well-preserved environment.

Suzhou Industrial Park is gearing up expansion into the east part of the city to gain more development space and satisfy its huge demand for land. [1] The move is part of the park's plan to build itself into a world leading international industrial park.

Pan Yunguan, deputy director of the management committee of Suzhou Industrial Park, said the expansion would be a milestone for the future of the park, which has become one of China's largest industrial parks in the past 11 years.

Already the biggest industrial park in the Yangtze River Delta region, it is projected to generate 250 billion yuan (US$30.8 billion) worth of GDP by 2014 with foreign and domestic investments exceeding US$100 billion. [2]

"The park is making a shift in its strategy to focus its future development in the east part of city, which is to the east of Gold Rooster Lake (Jin Ji Hu)," Pan said.

The park's administrative office moved east of the lake on the eve of the new year to serve the companies that intend to locate their manufacturing bases nearby. The expansion will help change the role of the park, which is not only a manufacturing base but a new city area with an important influence in the Yangtze River Delta region.[3]

Pan said the fledging east part of the facility will have a central business district and will welcome research institutes and companies in the service sectors, such as consulting, banking and logistics service. A 2-square-kilometre central business district is being built to the east of Gold Rooster Lake with shopping malls, entertainment facilities, food and beverage chain stores.

Mitsukoshi, Japan's largest department store chain, is planning to open its first store in the region according to www.ce.cn, a leading business news portal in China.

Ye Hua, general manager and senior consultant with Nomura Research Institute Shanghai Limited who is leading a team to conduct a development analysis for the park, echoed Pan.

"The park's future lies in its high-tech research capabilities, innovations and well-preserved environment when the foreign investment which powers the park flees for places with lower labour and material prices in the future,"[4] Ye told *China Daily* Shanghai and Delta. Ye also said the park has become a global manufacturing base for high-tech industry, which will help the park become a high-tech exporter. The list of companies that have established manufacturing and researching centres in the park include Japan Fujitu, South Korea Samsung and Netherlands Philips.

Economists and experts in the business predict a new boom in the park following the expansion.[5]

"The park will play an important role in the process when the city moves to the east to protect the ancient city area," said Ye. "Following the expansion, the central business district and shopping malls will be built in the area. As more and more people shop there, the old downtown will be free of the heavy traffic which will alleviate pressure on historic relics preservation."[6]

Real estate developers have rushed to the east. Genway Housing Development Group Co Ltd, a local real estate company, has sited its Fashion-City shopping malls to the east bank of the Gold Rooster Lake.

Notes

[1] Suzhou Industrial Park is gearing up expansion into the east part of the city to gain more development space and satisfy its huge demand for land.

【译文】苏州工业园区正在加速向城市东部扩张以获得更大的发展空间,满足其对土地的大量需求。

【解析】句中 gear up 有"换高速挡；促进；增加"等意思，根据这些基本意义，gearing up expansion 译作"加速扩张"是比较准确的。此外，还有短语 gear up for sth. 表示"（为某事）做好准备"，gear down 则是"换低速挡"的意思。

[2] Already the biggest industrial park in the Yangtze River Delta region, it is projected to generate 250 billion yuan (US$30.8 billion) worth of GDP by 2014 with foreign and domestic investments exceeding US$100 billion.

【译文】据推测，苏州工业园区作为目前长三角地区最大的工业园区，将在 2014 年创造 2500 亿元人民币（约 308 亿美元）的 GDP，并且国内外投资届时将超过 1000 亿美元。

【解析】the Yangtze River 是中国的"长江"，the Yangtze River Delta region 指的是"长江三角洲地区"，汉语里经常简称为"长三角地区"。

project 这里是"预计，推断"，it is projected 表示"据推测"，整个句子都是推测的内容，所以汉译时将"据推测"置于句首。

generate 是"产生，生成"的意思，而此处与之搭配使用的是"价值"，所以将其引申为"创造"，这样就比较合理。

翻译这个句子还应注意结尾处 with foreign and domestic investments exceeding US$100 billion 是指到 2014 年的时候国内外投资超过 1000 亿美元，所以参考译文中加入"届时"使时间更加明确，以免造成歧义。

[3] The expansion will help change the role of the park, which is not only a manufacturing base but a new city area with an important influence in the Yangtze River Delta region.

【译文】向东扩张将有助于园区的角色转换，使其不仅作为一个生产基地，也成为在长三角地区有重要影响的新城区。

【解析】句首 expansion 如果直译为"扩张"无可非议，但这里实际指的就是"向东扩张"，这也是全文的中心词，在翻译时把意义完整地表述出来更加符合商务语言的风格。

[4] The park's future lies in its high-tech research capabilities, innovations and well-preserved environment when the foreign investment which powers the park flees for places with lower labour and material prices in the future …

【译文】因为原本给园区注入活力的外国投资将来会流向劳动力和原材料价格更低的地区，园区的未来只有建立在高科技研发能力、创新能力以及对环境的妥善保护上。

【解析】power the park 译作"给园区注入活力"；flee 本意是"逃跑，逃走"，这里说的是"… investment … flees …"，所以译作"投资……流向……"符合汉语搭配习惯。原句用的是 when 引导的时间状语从句，但是因为主句和从句都比较长，如果翻译成汉语时也使用"当……的时候，园区的未来……"结构，会显得比较啰唆，逻辑也不是非常清晰，所以参考译文翻译成因果关系的句子，既符合原意，逻辑也一目了然。

[5] Economists and experts in the business predict a new boom in the park following the expansion.

【译文】这一领域的经济学家和专家预言,向东扩张将会给园区带来经济繁荣的新局面。

【解析】boom 是"繁荣,兴旺"的意思,既可作名词,也可作动词,该句中用作名词,作动词时如:

Business has been booming.

生意一直很兴隆。

[6] As more and more people shop there, the old downtown will be free of the heavy traffic which will alleviate pressure on historic relics preservation.

【译文】随着越来越多的人过去购物,老的商业中心将摆脱交通拥挤的状况,这也将缓解历史遗迹保护工作的压力。

【解析】downtown 既可作副词,意思是"在市区",也可作名词用,表示"市中心;商业区"。翻译 alleviate pressure on historic relics preservation 时,译文中增加了"工作"一词,因为英语中用词偏于抽象,汉语中偏向具体,alleviate pressure on historic relics preservation 实际就是指"缓解历史遗迹保护工作的压力"。

Passage B (English-Chinese Translation)

Action Speaks Louder than Words

Words & Expressions

Work on the following words and expressions and write the translated version in the space provided:

the primary stage of socialism	
serious imbalance in urban and rural development	
underdeveloped system	
a poor level of social fairness and justice	
economic restructuring	
the country's democratic and legal systems	
exclusive property	
political democracy	
respect for and obedience to core human values	
the belief and pursuit of democratic principles	
development level of productivity	
build a harmonious society	

In his recent article on China's historical tasks at the primary stage of socialism and its foreign policy, Premier Wen Jiabao acknowledges that the socialist system in China is still immature and has a large room for improvement. It was the first time a senior Chinese leader had published such a judgment. An editorial of *The Economic Observer*, a leading

Chinese business weekly, hails this as a breakthrough in guiding the country toward greater democracy and modernization.

When referring to China's underdevelopment at the current primary stage of socialism, Premier Wen Jiabao does not restrict the topic to such familiar economic issues as China's low per capita gross domestic product, its 20 million impoverished people and the serious imbalance in urban and rural development. He also emphasizes the underdevelopment in another area—that of "the immature socialist system".

Compared with low productivity, this underdeveloped system is a bigger obstacle to China's further development. [1] Yet, when modernizing China and improving the standard of living are discussed, economy and productivity are always the main focus. Obviously, this is not an objective posture.

The underdevelopment of the system is reflected in a poor level of social fairness and justice and in the limited channels to realize this, which are symptoms of the fact that reform in China's political system reform is lagging behind economic restructuring, and that the country's democratic and legal systems have yet to be improved. [2] What kind of road should we take to move China toward being a developed country?

Premier Wen says we should try to absorb and learn from all facets of human society and that science, democracy, rule of law, freedom, and human rights are not the exclusive property of capitalism. These are values the entire human race has been seeking throughout history, according to the premier. In this sense, the socialist system is not contradictory to political democracy.

Internally, whether the state system has become mature is reflected in whether it can ensure these common achievements and values of the human civilization, as well as major principles of political democracy, are shared by its people. [3] As is pointed out in Premier Wen's elaboration, the above-mentioned factors are the symbols of a mature socialist system. Externally, we believe that respect for and obedience to core human values, which are expounded by the premier, will help to eliminate the world's suspicion of China's peaceful development. Without a common outlook, it's impossible to have mutual trust. The belief and pursuit of democratic principles, which is based on such common values as freedom and the rule of law, is the most effective guarantee for China to overcome ideological differences, integrate with the international community and maintain peaceful relations with all other nations. [4]

Well-developed political democracy can be achieved only by continuous and steady reform of the current system. The significance of reform in China's political system is fully reflected in the words of the late Chinese leader Deng Xiaoping who said, "The success of all our other reforms depends on the success of the political reform." Chinese President Hu Jintao said during his visit to the United States in April 2006, "We always believe that without democracy, there is no modernization. Since it adopted the policy of reform and opening up, China has been not only trying to push forward its economic restructuring, but is also steadily pressing ahead with reforming its political system and granting its citizens more democratic rights and freedom."[5] Premier Wen also emphasizes that the development level of productivity is not the only criterion to measure the level of China's modernization. A developed country must be equipped with a well-developed democratic political system.

Admitting the immaturity of the current system shows our frankness and sincerity, but helping the socialist system become mature through reforms and improving the political democracy demand courage and selflessness.[6] Some critics say that China's political system reform has undergone three stages—"more words than deeds", "few words and few deeds" and the latest "more deeds than words". It is an over-simplistic criticism, but given the current social and economic development level, as well as the strategy of building a harmonious society and a harmonious world, it's time for us to say and do more.

Notes

[1] Compared with low productivity, the underdeveloped system is a bigger obstacle to China's further development.

【译文】跟低下的生产力相比,不发达的体制才是中国进一步发展的更大障碍。

【解析】compare with 意为"与……相比较",而 compare to 意为"比喻为……",要注意区分两种不同用法。

[2] The underdevelopment of the system is reflected in a poor level of social fairness and justice and in the limited channels to realize this, which are symptoms of the fact that reform in China's political system reform is lagging behind economic restructuring, and that the country's democratic and legal systems have yet to be improved.

【译文】社会公平和公正程度低以及实现公平和公正的渠道狭隘,不仅反映了体制的不发达,也体现了中国政治体制改革远远落后于经济改革,国家民主和法制体系尚有待于进一步改善。

【解析】a poor level of social fairness and justice 指"社会公平和公正程度低"。原句中虽然 the underdevelopment of the system 作主语,但仔细分析便可得知 a poor level of social fairness and justice and the limited channels to realize this 是连接主句和从句的关键,英语重主语,而汉语重主题,所以将该句译成中文时,应该把"社会公平和公正程度低以及实现公平和公正的渠道狭隘"这个主题提前。

[3] Internally, whether the state system has become mature is reflected in whether it can ensure these common achievements and values of the human civilization, as well as major principles of political democracy, are shared by its people.

【译文】从内部而言,国家体制是否成熟反映在这些共同的成就、人类文明的价值观以及政治民主的主要原则是否为全体人民所共享。

【解析】翻译这个句子时不需要调整语序,按照原句直译出来的汉语句子既符合原意,又通顺易懂。values of the human civilization 中以复数形式出现的 values 表示"价值观念;行为标准"。

[4] The belief and pursuit of democratic principles, which is based on such common values as freedom and the rule of law, is the most effective guarantee for China to overcome ideological differences, integrate with the international community and maintain peaceful relations with all other nations.

【译文】建立在自由和法治这类共同价值观基础之上的对民主原则的信仰和追求,是中国克服意识形态的差异、与国际社会接轨以及维护与他国之间和平关系的最有力的保证。

【解析】guarantee 除了"保证"这个意思外,还表示"商品使用保证,保修期;担保"。overcome ideological differences, integrate with the international community and maintain peaceful relations with all other nations 这几个短语都是跟中国有关的政治经济文本中经常提到的,译文比较固定,翻译这类词句时最好不要随便改动译文。

[5] We always believe that without democracy, there is no modernization. Since it adopted the policy of reform and opening up, China has been not only trying to push forward its economic restructuring, but is also steadily pressing ahead with reforming its political system and granting its citizens more democratic rights and freedom.

【译文】我们始终相信没有民主就没有现代化。自改革开放政策实施以来,中国不仅一直努力推进经济改革,而且也在稳步推进政治体制改革以赋予公民更多的民主权利和自由。

【解析】push forward 和 press ahead 都是"推进,推动"的意思,如果两个地方都译成"推进"会显得语言单调乏味,所以为了使语言富于变化,译文中两处用了不同的表达。grant 是"授予,赋予;承认"的意思,这里译为"赋予公民权利和自由"。

[6] Admitting the immaturity of the current system shows our frankness and sincerity, but helping the socialist system become mature through reforms and improving the political democracy demand courage and selflessness.

【译文】承认当前体系的不成熟体现出我们的诚恳与坦率,但是通过改革来帮助社会主义制度走向成熟以及改善政治民主都需要极大的勇气和忘我精神。

【解析】句尾 demand courage and selflessness 中的 selflessness 是"忘我,无私"的意思,如果直译成"需要勇气和忘我",不符合汉语表达习惯,因为汉语注重具体,所以增译成"忘我精神"更加准确。

Passage C (Chinese-English Translation)

中国经济在世界经济中的作用

进入21世纪,特别是中国打破重重阻挠加入WTO以后,中国经济在世界经济中的作用已被世人瞩目。由于世界生产链的重新分工和转移,中国成为世界上一个制造大国,进而带动了许多发展中国家经济的发展,它们向中国出口资源、农产品和制造业半成品,中国也向全世界提供价廉物美的工业品。

英国《经济学家》2005年7月30日这一期,分析了中国经济在世界经济上的地位和作用,认为"中国几乎推动着世界经济正在发生的一切","全球通胀率、利率、国债收益率、房地产价格、工资、利润和商品价格现在越来越受中国政策的驱动,这可能成为至少半个世纪以来世界上最深刻的经济变化"。

中国实行改革开放政策28年来,中国经济保持了9.4%的增长速度,并且在诸多领域取得了骄人的成绩。中国的社会主义制度得到了加强,因为它把社会主义的基本社会制度和市场经济体制恰当地结合了起来;生产力得到了空前发展,人民生活水平得到了显著提高;综合国力显著增长,经济结构有了调整。因而在世界经济中的地位有了提升,成为世界经济向前发展的一种推动力。

Translation Skills(Ⅵ)

翻译中的语序调整

语言是思维的外壳,思维方式不同,语言表达习惯就不同。汉语民族和英语民族在各自漫长的历史发展过程中,形成了各自独特的思维方式,因此往往会对同一事物或观点有不同的语言传达顺序。比如修饰中心词时,汉语中修饰语多置于中心词之前,而英语中修饰语多置于中心词之后;汉语多采用主动句式和正常语序句,而英语多用被动句式和倒装句式;表达因果、假设等关系时,汉语多先因后果,先假设后结论,而英语恰恰相反;汉语重"从大到小"、从整体到个体,英语重"从小到大"、从特殊到普遍;有时汉英语句排列顺序的不同完全是约定俗成,很难用什么理由来解释。译者能够了解两种语言在语序上的差异,在英汉互译过程中,根据译入语的表达习惯适当调整语序,就会更好地传达原文的意思,促进翻译质量的提高。下面将从几个译例分析中总结出几种常见的英汉语序差异以及英汉翻译过程中语序调整的手段和方法。

一、定语语序的调整

例1 Court Martial 军事法庭 Consul General 总领事

汉语中单个单词作定语修饰中心词时,放在中心词之前,英语中一般也是如此。但有时英语中会将定语后置,如例1所示,在英译汉时就要调整语序,将定语置于汉语中心词之前。

例2 Trade in leather has gone up (down) 3%.

译文：皮革贸易上升(下降)了3%。

例3　His advice about tight cash management and cost reduction has been noted.

译文：他关于紧缩银根降低成本的建议引起了注意。

若是短语或从句作定语,在汉语中它们一般置于中心词前,而英语更倾向于后置。例2和例3中,英语短语作定语修饰中心词时都后置,在汉语译文中,这些短语修饰语都被移至中心词之前。

例4　我们要把中国建设成为社会主义的现代化强国。

译文：China will be developed to a modern powerful socialist country.

如果中心词由几个定语来修饰时,汉语习惯把最能表明事物本质的放在最前,表示规模大小、力量强弱的放在最后,英语则是越能表明事物本质的定语越靠近中心词。因此,英汉互译时遇到多个定语修饰同一中心词的句子时,要对定语语序进行调整。

二、状语语序的调整

例1　本公司将于3月1日在银行家俱乐部召开股东年会。

译文：The annual general meeting of the shareholders of our company will be held at the Bankers' Club on March 1.

例2　他每天早上在户外高声朗读。

译文：He reads aloud in the open every morning.

从以上两个例子可以看出,英汉状语的语序排列也有很大差异。当一个英语句子中出现多重状语时,翻译成汉语时的语序一般表现为时间状语—地点状语—方式状语,而英语则正好相反。

三、时间、空间关系上的语序调整

例1　他出生于1980年7月13日凌晨2点。

译文：He was born at 2:00 o'clock on July 13th, 1980.

例2　中国江苏省苏州市十梓街1号

译文：1# Shizi Street, Suzhou, Jiangsu Province, China

例3　她目前就读于苏州大学外国语学院英语系。

译文：She is now studying in English Department of School of Foreign Languages, Soochow University.

汉语重"从大到小",英语重"从小到大"。汉语的思维是由远及近,由重至轻,从普遍到特殊,从主观到客观,从整体到个体。英语思维方式则是从小到大,由近及远,先轻后重,从特殊到普遍,从个体到整体;这种思维上的差异性对语言表达有直接影响。从上面的例1、例2和例3中可以看出,汉语一个句子中出现多个时间单位或空间单位时,常按从大到小、从宽到窄、从远到近的顺序排列;英语则同汉语大体相反。

四、因果关系句及假设关系句的语序调整

例1　They decided to give up the trip because it looked like rain.

译文：因为可能下雨,所以他们决定不出去了。

例 2　I shall do it tomorrow if I have time.

译文：如果我有时间,明天就做。

汉语的逻辑性很强,它的语序主要靠逻辑思维而定,通常根据一定的逻辑顺序按照由原因到结果、由假设到推论、由条件到结果的次序,有先有后、有主有次地逐层叙述;而英语的语序比较灵活,通常开门见山,直奔主题,先说结果再说原因或先说结论后说假设。

五、倒装句和被动句的语序调整

例 1　Only by working hard can we achieve the aim.

译文：只有通过努力工作,我们才能达到目标。

例 2　Never had he had any experience like that.

译文：他从来没有经历过那种事。

英语中经常使用倒装句,汉语则不然。英语倒装句的形式多种多样,比如例 1 中副词 only 置于句首时的倒装,例 2 以否定副词 never 开头的强调否定句的倒装,再比如疑问句、there be 句型、某些让步状语从句的倒装等。将英语倒装句译成汉语时,通常按照正常的语序来翻译。

例 3　Our trade is conducted on the basis of equality.

译文：我们在平等的基础上进行贸易。

例 4　同时,两国显著扩大了文化交流与贸易往来。

译文：At the same time, trade and cultural exchanges between the two countries have been notably expanded.

英语中被动语态使用比较频繁,而汉语中主动语态使用更为普遍。在英汉互译时,应该根据译入语的表达习惯调整语序。

六、句子中既有叙事又有表态时的语序调整

例 1　I am glad to see you.

译文：见到你很高兴。

例 2　It is important to finish the project on time.

译文：按时完工很重要。

例 3　It was a keen disappointment when I had to postpone the visit to China, which I intended to pay in January.

译文：我原打算一月份访问中国,后来不得不推迟,这使我深感遗憾。

一个句子如果既有叙事部分又有表态部分,在英语里一般都是先表明态度或说出个人感受,然后再叙述有关事实或情况;而汉语往往先把事物或情况讲清楚,最后再说出感受,进行表态或评论。

七、习惯表达法的语序调整

东南西北 north and south, east and west
前后 back and forth
新旧 old and new

水陆 land and water
田径 track and field
迟早 sooner or later
血肉 flesh and blood
饮食 eat and drink
螺旋式通货膨胀 inflationary spiral

汉语和英语有许多约定俗成的习惯性表达方式,其中有的语序正好相反。译者只有熟悉这些约定俗成的习惯表达,在翻译时调整语序,才能使译文符合译入语的表达习惯。

通过以上举例分析,我们可以比较清楚地了解英汉语序常见的异同之处。总之,在英汉互译时,我们应该根据语义和语境灵活合理地调整语序,尽可能使译文既准确传达原文的意义,又顺应译入语的表达习惯。

Translation Exercises

1. The IMF projected a slight decline in the rate of output growth in the industrial countries.
2. The World Bank loans are expected to generate economic development, which eventually provides the source for repayment.
3. The company is gearing up for the big export drive.
4. The central government will grant more financial support to these regions.
5. 要是你把他俩的工作比较一下,就会发现他的好多了。(compare)
6. 如果我能从银行贷到5万美元,你愿意给我当担保人吗?(guarantee)
7. 中国的经济繁荣反过来也给世界提供了一个广大的市场。(boom)
8. 那家公司能采取什么措施来缓解这个问题呢?(alleviate)

Passage A　(English-Chinese Translation)

The Circular Economy Concept

Words & Expressions

Work on the following words and expressions and write the translated version in the space provided:

circular economy _____
resource optimization _____
emission of pollutants _____
eco-chains _____
cleaner production _____
bio-refineries _____
discarded biomass _____
throw-away habits _____
maximum efficiency of resource-use _____
eco-industrial parks and networks _____

The Circular Economy approach to resource-use efficiency integrates cleaner production and industrial ecology in a broader system encompassing industrial firms, networks or chains of firms, eco-industrial parks, and regional infrastructure to support resource optimization.[1] State-owned and private enterprises, government and private infrastructure, and consumers all have a role in achieving the CE. The three basic levels of action are:
- At the individual firm level, managers must seek much higher efficiency through the three Rs of CE, reduce consumption of resources and emission of pollutants and waste, reuse resources, and recycle by-products.[2] (Sustainable product and process design is important in German and Japanese recycling economy plans but is just emerging as a component of the Chinese CE concept.)
- The second level is to reuse and recycle resources within industrial parks and

clustered or chained industries, so that resources will circulate fully in the local production system. (The Chinese use the term "eco-chains" for by-product exchanges.)
- The third level is to integrate different production and consumption systems in a region so the resources circulate among industries and urban systems. This level requires development of municipal or regional by-product collection, storage, processing, and distribution systems.

Efforts at all three levels include development of resource recovery and cleaner production enterprises and public facilities to support realization of the CE concept. This adds a strong economic development dimension through investment in new ventures and job creation.[3] So the CE opens opportunities for both domestic and foreign enterprises.

A logical extension of the third regional level of action would be integrating management of flows among urban, suburban, and rural resource recovery systems.[4] An example would be bio-refineries utilizing discarded biomass from rural and urban sources. Such refineries would operate with a range of technologies for converting these resources into bio-energy, bio-fuel, and bio-materials.

Consumers have a role at the household and neighborhood level in applying the CE concept. The majority of the Chinese people still fail to meet all of their basic material needs, including potable water for drinking and sanitation, affordable and good quality food, basic housing, and household equipment. The Circular Economy must support families in achieving these requirements of life. At the same time local initiatives must offer citizens education in the practices of reduce, reuse, and recycle at the home level.[5]

Once basic needs are met, CE leaders are aware of the challenge involved in shifting to less material consumption patterns, one that improves quality of life and avoids the Western lifestyle of wasteful consumption and "throw-away habits". However, given the present level of poverty, the main focus is on meeting basic needs through maximum efficiency of resource-use.

The Circular Economy concept brings together cleaner production and industrial ecology with its application as eco-industrial development.[6] Circular Economy plans, such as ones completed in Liaoning and Jiangsu Provinces, call for development of eco-industrial parks and networks as central strategies. However, a very partial definition of EIP usually limits it to "one company uses the wastes of another". This misses the systematic understanding of how such parks can support the achievements of the Circular Economy in a region.

Notes

[1] The Circular Economy approach to resource-use efficiency integrates cleaner production and industrial ecology in a broader system encompassing industrial

firms, networks or chains of firms, eco-industrial parks, and regional infrastructure to support resource optimization.

【译文】循环经济在一个包含了工业公司、公司网或公司链、生态工业区以及地区基础设施在内的广泛体系下,将清洁生产和工业生态学相结合,以获得资源利用效率,从而支持资源的最优化。

【解析】cleaner production 译作"清洁生产"。清洁生产是指将综合预防的环境保护策略持续应用于生产过程和产品中,以期减少对人类和环境的风险。
optimization 意为"最优化,最佳化"。

[2] At the individual firm level, managers must seek much higher efficiency through the three Rs of CE, reduce consumption of resources and emission of pollutants and waste, reuse resources, and recycle by-products.

【译文】从单个公司的层面来讲,管理人员必须通过循环经济的"三 R"原则(即"减量化,再使用,再循环"三原则)来减少资源消耗以及污染物和废弃物的排放,对资源进行再使用,使副产品得到再循环,以此寻求更高的效率。

【解析】该句中 the three Rs of CE 译作"循环经济的'三 R'原则",即"减量化(reduce),再使用(reuse),再循环(recycle)"。

[3] This adds a strong economic development dimension through investment in new ventures and job creation.

【译文】通过对新项目进行投资和创造就业机会扩大了经济发展空间。

【解析】dimension 原意是"尺寸;方面;维数",这里理解为"由新项目投资和就业机会扩大带来的经济发展空间"。

[4] A logical extension of the third regional level of action would be integrating management of flows among urban, suburban, and rural resource recovery systems.

【译文】对城市、郊区以及乡村资源回收系统实行一体化的管理流程是对循环经济概念实施的第三个层面,即地区实施水平的合理延伸。

【解析】文中把循环经济概念的实施分成三个层面:第一层是在个体公司的实施,第二层是在工业园区或产业链内的实施,第三层就是在一个地区内的实施,所以在翻译 the third regional level of action 时,增译为"循环经济概念实施的第三个层面,即地区实施水平",使表达更加明确。

[5] At the same time local initiatives must offer citizens education in the practices of reduce, reuse, and recycle at the home level.

【译文】同时,地方倡导者必须为当地居民挨家挨户提供减量化、再利用、再循环的实践教育。

【解析】initiative 原本指"主动的行为,首创精神",这里不可以直译,因为能够提供教育的必须是人或是机构,不可能是行为或精神,所以将其译作"倡导者"。
at the home level 意思是"为每家每户都提供教育",所以用"挨家挨户"符合句意。

[6] The Circular Economy concept brings together cleaner production and industrial ecology with its application as eco-industrial development.

【译文】循环经济概念将清洁生产和工业生态学结合运用到生态工业发展中。

【解析】该句译文将 with its application as eco-industrial development 译作"运用到生态工业发展中",把英语中的 application 这一名词转化为汉语中的动词,使译文更加符合汉语表达习惯。

Passage B (English-Chinese Translation)

The Awareness Motivating the Circular Economy

Words & Expressions

Work on the following words and expressions and write the translated version in the space provided:

depletion of natural resources

degradation of major ecosystems

unsustainable model of development

The State Environmental Protection Administration of China (SEPA)

China Council for International Co-operation on Environment and Development (CCICED)

the all-round well-being society

seven-fold increase

parallel objective of reducing pollution

aggressive industrialization

inequity in distribution of wealth and income

massive instability and unrest

China's rapid industrialization in the last decades has engendered serious problems of depletion of natural resources, degradation of major ecosystems, and pollution extending far beyond its borders.[1] (Economy 2004, Pan Yue 2004) Projections by the country's top leadership have persuaded key officials that continuing this unsustainable model of development is simply not possible. The resources are not available to provide a growing population with higher standards in a Western lifestyle of consumption. The challenge for the Chinese government and people is to create an alternative to Western economic development models. This alternative must enable social and political stability in a time of economic dislocation and growing expectations.[2]

The State Environmental Protection Administration of China (SEPA), and the China Council for International Co-operation on Environment and Development (CCICED), have directed the attention of the top leaders of China, at both national and local levels, to a hard reality: the development target set by the government will not be achieved unless alternative models of economic development are identified and applied.[3]

This ambitious development target is to raise the majority of China's population into "the all-round well-being society". This means that by 2050 a larger population of 1.8 billion would reach a per capita GDP of US$4,000 per year, five times the current level. Some estimate that this increase could occur within the next 30 years. This demands a tremendous increase in production and multiplies pressure on natural resources and the environment. Research by the State Environmental Protection Administration indicates that China's economy will need to achieve at least a seven-fold increase in efficiency of resource use to achieve the goals set for 2050, while maintaining environmental quality.[4] The CCICED states that an increase as much as ten-fold will be required (Lei and Qian 2003).

The need for the parallel objective of reducing pollution is directly experienced in the provinces, cities, and countryside. Five decades of aggressive industrialization has seriously degraded all natural resources. The Natural Capital accounts for current and future generations show the massive debits of polluted rivers, cleared mountains, depleted soil, and coal and steel mine sites full of toxic materials.[5]

With China's opening up to foreign investment and increasing inequity in distribution of wealth and income, more and more Chinese are demanding a better life: jobs and higher income as well as a better environment to live in. State ministers, provincial governors and city mayors are feeling the pressure for development. They are acutely aware of China's regular periods of massive instability and unrest. They need to meet the demand for improved quality of life to assure political and economic stability.[6]

To meet the needs for development while restoring the health of ecosystems, the only option is to follow a development path different from the industrialization model of the West. China's leaders see that continuing the present massive exploitation of natural resources and inefficient production practices cannot continue. They also are aware that a US life-style emphasizing material possessions is simply not achievable. Their conclusion is to adopt the Japanese and German Recycling Economy approaches and set higher goals than either.

Notes

[1] China's rapid industrialization in the last decades has engendered serious problems of depletion of natural resources, degradation of major ecosystems, and pollution extending far beyond its borders.

【译文】中国过去几十年工业化的飞速发展已造成自然资源耗尽、主要生态系统退化、环境污染过度等严重问题。

【解析】 depletion 是"耗尽"的意思,动词形式为 deplete,如 deplete a country of its natural resources 意为"耗尽一个国家的自然资源";degradation 是"退化;降级"的意思;句尾 pollution extending far beyond its borders 字面意义是"超出界限的污染",为了与前面句式保持一致,所以意译为"环境污染过度"。

[2] This alternative must enable social and political stability in a time of economic dislocation and growing expectations.

【译文】 在经济混乱、期望值不断增长的年代,这个可供选择的模式必须能够保证社会和政治的稳定。

【解析】 alternative 作名词,原意是"变通办法;供选择的东西",从上文中可知,这里的 alternative 是指"可供选择的经济发展模式"。

译文中对原句的语序进行了调整,将原句末的状语放在了句首,使译文符合汉语习惯。

[3] ... to a hard reality: the development target set by the government will not be achieved unless alternative models of economic development are identified and applied.

【译文】 ……引向一个严峻的现实:除非这一可供选择的经济发展模式确立并得到实施,否则政府设定的发展目标不可能实现。

【解析】 identify 在这里理解为"确立",它还可表示"识别,鉴定,认出"等意义。

原句中先说结论,后说条件,为了符合汉语先说条件、后说结论的逻辑表达习惯,译文对语序作了调整。

[4] Research by the State Environmental Protection Administration indicates that China's economy will need to achieve at least a seven-fold increase in efficiency of resource use to achieve the goals set for 2050, while maintaining environmental quality.

【译文】 国家环境保护总局的研究表明,中国经济要想实现为 2050 年设定的目标,就必须在保持环境质量不变的同时使资源利用率至少实现七倍的增长。

【解析】 State Environmental Protection Administration 是指中国的"国家环境保护总局"。

[5] The Natural Capital accounts for current and future generations show the massive debits of polluted rivers, cleared mountains, depleted soil, and coal and steel mine sites full of toxic materials.

【译文】 当代人和子孙后代赖以生存的自然资本账户上已经欠债很多:到处都是受到污染的河流、光秃的山脉、消耗殆尽的土地以及充满有毒物质的煤矿和铁矿。

【解析】 account for 是"说明"的意思;debit 是会计术语,意为"借记",可引申为欠账。这里是比喻用法,表明人类社会的经济活动给自然环境造成了巨大的破坏,相当于人类对自己所生存的环境欠下了一笔债。

[6] They need to meet the demand for improved quality of life to assure political and economic stability.

【译文】 他们必须满足人们对更高生活质量的需求才能确保政治和经济的稳定。

【解析】 quality of life 通常译作"生活质量",improved quality of life 是指"改善了的生活质量",得到改善的生活质量其实就是更高的生活质量。

Passage C (Chinese-English Translation)

什么是循环经济？

循环经济是由美国经济学家波尔丁在20世纪60年代首先提出的。所谓循环经济(circular economy)，即在经济发展中，遵循生态学规律，将清洁生产、资源综合利用、生态设计和可持续消费等融为一体，使经济系统和自然生态系统的物质和谐循环，维护自然生态的平衡。

循环经济内涵"3R"原则：减量化(Reduce)，尽量减少资源的开采量和使用量；再使用(Reuse)，资源开采后尽量地使用、再使用，增加频率，拉长使用时间；再循环(Recycle)，当不能再使用时，设法将它变成再生资源，循环到社会中去。循环经济与线性经济相区别。线性经济即所谓传统经济模式，即资源开采—生产部门—消费部门—废弃(污染)，是一种直线性的消耗模式。而循环经济则强调循环，资源变为成品被消费后形成的废品应可以再循环。发达国家的循环经济较发达，如可以实现钢45%的原料再生率，铜实现了62.3%的原料再生率，纸的再生率也达35%。

循环经济包含三个层次：第一层次是企业内的物质循环—符合循环经济发展要求的典型企业。第二层次是企业之间的物质循环—符合循环经济发展要求的生态工业(农业)园区。第三层次是包括生产和消费的整个过程的物质循环—资源节约型、环境友好型城市。

Translation Exercises

1. "Time service" meets the needs of people at a time when the pace of living has accelerated and the concept of consumption is changing.
2. Limited liability tends to make the corporation an attractive alternative for investors.
3. To make good use of what we have, we must optimize the distribution of raw materials.
4. To debit an account means to enter an amount on the left or debit side of the account.
5. 他觉得分配给他那么小的一间办公室是在贬低他的身份。(degrade)
6. 我们需要确定最佳的解决方法。(identify)
7. 那个项目几乎耗尽了那家公司的财力。(deplete)
8. 已经向当地工商管理局申请营业执照。(application)

Unit 14

Passage A (English-Chinese Translation)

Obtaining Scale Economies
David A. AAKER

Words & Expressions

Work on the following words and expressions and write the translated version in the space provided:

scale economies   _____
product standardization   _____
advertising theme   _____
advertising production costs   _____
demand and fashion patterns   _____
create a dominant position   _____
form a consortium with ...   _____
export centers   _____

Scale economies can occur from product standardization. The Ford world-car concept, for example, allows product design, tooling, parts production, and product testing to be spread over a much larger sales base. [1] Standardization of the development and execution of a marketing program can also be an important source of scale economies. Consider Coca-Cola, which since the 1950s has employed a marketing strategy—the brand name, concentrate formula, positioning, and advertising theme—that has been virtually the same throughout the world. Only the artificial sweetener and packaging differ across countries. Brands such as Smirnoff, Pantene Pro-V, Nike, and Disney have saved significant advertising production costs by using the same advertising themes and executions across countries even when the executions are tailored to the local market. [2]

Several influential observers have suggested that the SCAs emerging from worldwide scale economies are becoming more important and that in many industries they are becoming a necessary aspect of being competitive. [3] Theodore Levitt, in a visible and now classic article on the globalization of markets, posits that worldwide communications have caused demand and fashion patterns to be similar across the world, even in less developed countries. Kenichi Ohmae, longtime head of McKinsey in Japan and the author of several classic books and articles on global business, cites a litany of products that are virtually identical in Japan, Europe, and the United States, including Nike footwear, Pampers diapers, Band-Aid bandages, Cheer detergent, Nestlé coffee, Kodak film, Revlon cosmetics, and Contac paper. He notes that people from different countries, from youths to business people, wear the same fashions.

Ohmae also suggests that the long-accepted waterfall model of international trade is now obsolete. In this model, a firm first establishes itself in a domestic market. It then penetrates the markets of other advanced countries before moving into less developed countries. The experience of Honda in motorcycles is representative. After creating a dominant position in Japan with considerable scale economies, it entered the US market by convincing people that it was fun to ride its small, simple motorcycle and by investing in a 2000-dealer network.[4] With its scale economies thus increased, Honda expanded its line to include larger cycles and then moved into the European market.

The new model, according to Ohmae, is that of a sprinkler, which exposes a product all over the globe at once. He points to products such as the Sony Walkman, Canon's AE-1, and the Minolta A-7000, which exploded onto the worldwide market in a matter of months. The Walkman actually first took off in California. Under the sprinkler model, a firm introducing a new product doesn't have time to develop a presence and distribution channel in a foreign market. Instead, it forms a consortium with other firms that have already established distribution in other countries. This allows the new product to go global immediately. The resulting economies of scale can allow lower prices, often a key to creating markets and a barrier to competitors.[5]

In order to achieve maximum scale economies, a manufacturer would need to make all units in its home country. Yet, for many reasons, companies spread component production and final assembly throughout the world.[6] Matsushita, which has 150 plants in 38 countries, has developed export centers as a way to gain the advantages of politically hospitable, low-cost host countries close to regional markets that will support substantial economies of scale. The export center does more than simply manufacture a product. It controls the product from the drawing board to the loading dock. The Malaysian export center, one of the first, produces one quarter of Matsushita's air-conditioner and TV revenue.

Notes

[1]   The Ford world-car concept, for example, allows product design, tooling, parts

production, and product testing to be spread over a much larger sales base.

【译文】比如说,福特造世界汽车的概念允许产品设计、加工、零部件生产以及产品测试能够覆盖更加广阔的销售基础。

【解析】tooling 意思是"加工";spread over 表示"遍布在……,覆盖在……"。

[2] Brands such as Smirnoff, Pantene Pro-V, Nike, and Disney have saved significant advertising production costs by using the same advertising themes and executions across countries even when the executions are tailored to the local market.

【译文】如司木露、潘婷、耐克和迪斯尼等品牌通过在不同国家使用同一广告主题和制作省下了大笔的广告成本,即使这一广告是根据当地市场需求量身定做的。

【解析】execution 在该句中是"制作;手法"的意思,但在大多数情况下,execution 表示"执行,实施"这个意思,如:

We assure you of the punctual execution of your order.

我方保证准时执行你方订单。

tailor to 意思是"使适合……的需要",译文中将 are tailored to the local market 译作"是根据当地市场需求量身定做的",既符合原意,又生动形象。

[3] Several influential observers have suggested that the SCAs emerging from worldwide scale economies are becoming more important and that in many industries they are becoming a necessary aspect of being competitive.

【译文】一些有影响力的观察家暗示,从世界范围内的规模经济发展而来的可持续竞争优势变得越来越重要,而且在许多行业中正成为保持竞争力的必要条件。

【解析】SCAs = sustainable competitive advantages,意为"可持续竞争优势"。

competitive 意为"竞争的,有竞争力的",如:

Our firm offers you competitive prices.

我们公司给你所报的价格很有竞争力。

[4] After creating a dominant position in Japan with considerable scale economies, it entered the US market by convincing people that it was fun to ride its small, simple motorcycle and by investing in a 2000-dealer network.

【译文】以可观的规模经济在日本占据主导地位之后,本田汽车公司使人们相信驾驶他们的小型轻便摩托车是一件有趣的事,并且投资建立了一个由2000名经销商组成的网络,从而成功地打入了美国市场。

【解析】dominant position 意为"主导地位";considerable 意为"相当大的,可观的"。

small, simple motorcycle 中 simple 译成"轻便的"而非"简单的"。

invest sth. (in)意为"投资;投入",如:

The bank invested heavily in automobile industry.

那家银行在汽车工业中投资很多。

[5] The resulting economies of scale can allow lower prices, often a key to creating markets and a barrier to competitors.

【译文】由此产生的规模经济允许产品低价售出,而低价不仅是创造市场的关键,也给竞争对手筑起了一道屏障。

[6]　　Yet, for many reasons, companies spread component production and final assembly throughout the world.

【译文】然而,因为多方面的原因,公司将部件生产和最终装配分布到世界各地。

【解析】component 意为"部件,组件";final assembly 意为"最终装配",而 assembly line 则是"流水(装配)线"的意思。

Passage B　(English-Chinese Translation)

Wealth on the Wing
Marc Faber

Words & Expressions

Work on the following words and expressions and write the translated version in the space provided:

global economic expansion	_____
manufactured goods	_____
price gains for commodities	_____
loose monetary policy	_____
current-account deficits	_____
real per-capita income gains	_____
adjust for inflation	_____
emerging economies	_____
geopolitical power	_____
engines of growth	_____
have a significant overweight position	_____

　　The current global economic expansion, which began in the US in November 2001, is unusual in one major aspect: for the first time in modern history, China and increasingly India, the world's two most populous countries, are factors in the global economy. Nobody paid any attention to them during economic recoveries in 1975, 1982 and 1991. But today, China, which recently became the world's fourth largest economy, has great significance both as a supplier of manufactured goods and a consumer of natural resources. The demand from China for raw materials has already resulted in higher equilibrium prices for many commodities, from coal to copper to palm oil. And if all goes well in India, which has many economic similarities to China 20 years ago, its economy will clock real GDP growth of more than 7% a year for the next decade, driving further price gains for commodities.[1]

　　The implications of the rise of China and India go far beyond higher palm-oil prices.

There's another, less talked about, shift going on that will profoundly influence investment returns in global markets over the coming years. Since the late 1990s, the US has been on a borrowing and spending binge, aided by low interest rates and very loose monetary policy. [2] As a result, it's running record trade and current-account deficits, particularly with its Asian trading partners, which conversely are running bulging trade and current-account surpluses. Put another way: while the US has been busy consuming (and borrowing heavily to do so), Asia—and China in particular—has been investing in factories and technologies so it can produce even more goods and services to sell abroad.

This scenario has a predictable outcome. Large numbers of Asians are experiencing real per-capita income gains exceeding those in the developed world. Indeed, in the US and Western Europe, median per-capita incomes adjusted for inflation have barely increased in the past 20 years; in China, the median income has doubled every 10 years since the country began opening up its economy in 1978.

A huge shift of wealth and power to Asia is thus taking place, leading to an unprecedented situation in economic history. [3] In the past, it was always the rich countries that financed economic development in emerging economies. European capital built canals and railroads in the 19th century US economy; in the 20th century, European and American money bankrolled development in Latin America, Australia and Asia. But today, it's the poor countries—notably China—that are financing American consumption by purchasing US government bonds. No wonder that with their vast liquidity, stock markets in many developing countries have vastly outperformed the US market. [4] Since lows reached in October 2002, America's S&P 500 index has risen 50%, while indexes in India and Jakarta are up by more than 300%.

This trend is likely to persist, in part because it isn't just wealth that's moving from West to East. Each time manufacturing and services are outsourced to Asia, knowledge, technology and skills are also transferred. [5] Professor Richard Smalley, a Nobel-Prize-winning chemist at Rice University, estimated that by 2010, 90% of all Ph. Ds in physical science and engineering may be living in Asia. With economic prowess comes geopolitical power. For many countries, exports to China have replaced exports to the US as engines of growth—one reason why a longtime US ally like South Korea is cozying up to China. [6] Moreover, China's appetite for raw materials (and India's hunger in the future) is shifting political power from industrialized countries to resource-rich ones, giving leaders like Mahmoud Ahmadinejad, Hugo Chávez and Vladimir Putin extra clout.

Investors must understand that the current changes in economic geography, wealth and geopolitical power, while associated with greater geopolitical risks, also offer huge opportunities in emerging economies. They are the prime beneficiaries of the demise of the communist and socialist ideology, the invention of instant and free communication, and efficient transportation and distribution, as well as easy US monetary policies. Investors would do well to have a significant overweight position in countries as diverse as Thailand, Malaysia, Vietnam, and Singapore, which are likely to significantly outperform the US over the next few years.

Notes

[1]　And if all goes well in India, which has many economic similarities to China 20 years ago, its economy will clock real GDP growth of more than 7% a year for the next decade, driving further price gains for commodities.

【译文】印度目前的经济状况与20年前的中国有许多相似之处,如果一切进展顺利的话,今后10年印度国内生产总值年增长将超过7%,同时会进一步推高商品价格。

【解析】clock real GDP growth 中的 clock 指"达到(所说时间、距离或速度)",如:
He clocked 9.6 seconds in the 100 metres.
他用9.6秒跑完100米。
clock real GDP growth of more than 7%意思是"GDP年增长超过7%"。

[2]　Since the late 1990s, the US has been on a borrowing and spending binge, aided by low interest rates and very loose monetary policy.

【译文】20世纪90年代末以来,由于低利率和宽松的货币政策,美国一直处于借款和消费的热潮中。

【解析】binge 意思是"无节制的狂热行动",a buying binge 表示"无节制的购买",a shopping binge 指"购买热"。
loose monetary policy 指"宽松的货币政策",与之相对应的说法则是 tight money policy(紧缩银根政策)。

[3]　A huge shift of wealth and power to Asia is thus taking place, leading to an unprecedented situation in economic history.

【译文】目前,财富和权力正在向亚洲转移,这种情况在经济史上是前所未有的。

[4]　No wonder that with their vast liquidity, stock markets in many developing countries have vastly outperformed the US market.

【译文】由于许多发展中国家流动性很强,发展中国家的股票比美国的股票更为走俏便不足为奇。

【解析】liquidity 意思是"流动性;资产折现力"。
outperform 本意是"胜过,做得比……好",商务英语中通常用来描述股票,如 a stock that outperformed all others 意思是"比所有其他股票更为走俏的股票"。

[5]　Each time manufacturing and services are outsourced to Asia, knowledge, technology and skills are also transferred.

【译文】每次生产和服务被外包到亚洲,知识、技术和技能也同时发生了转移。

【解析】outsourcing 在商务英语中是"外部采办,外购"的意思,通常简称为"外包",指公司原自行制造的部件改向外国或国内不承认工会的供货商采购。
transfer 是"转移"的意思,形容词形式 transferable 表示"可转让的"。

[6]　For many countries, exports to China have replaced exports to the US as engines of

growth—one reason why a longtime US ally like South Korea is cozying up to China.

【译文】对许多国家来说,对中国的出口已经取代了对美国的出口,并成为经济增长的动力,这也是为什么像韩国这样的美国的长期合作伙伴正在转而向中国讨好。

【解析】cozy up to 意思是"低三下四地与……攀交情;拼命巴结,向……讨好"。

Passage C (Chinese-English Translation)

中国企业海外"本土化"战略

全面提升本企业的核心竞争力,并推动企业的国际化发展步伐,是中国企业家梦寐以求的目标。中资企业能否实现海外"本土化",是我国海外企业能否生存和发展的关键。"本土化"首先要求投资者在观念上实现"本土化"。只有这样,才能实现人才、营销等方面的"本土化"。如果将观念划入企业文化范畴,那么可以毫不夸张地说,企业文化的"本土化"是企业跨国经营成败的关键。其实,中国企业要学习跨国经营的"本土化",我们身边就有最好的老师,譬如:可口可乐在品牌推广方面采用中国传统十二生肖贺岁包装,以中国人熟悉和喜爱的名人做广告代言人等策略。

中国企业海外投资的"本土化",可以相对缓解国内企业进入国际市场的三个难题。一是消费者对外来品牌的抵触心理;二是进入国的非关税贸易壁垒;三是国际商务人才的匮乏。就海外投资能力而言,中国并非强国,而是弱国,其可支配的资金、技术、人才都十分有限,但是以"本土化"的方式运作,就可以更好地弥补我们在这方面的不足。作为中国企业国际化的先行者,海尔国际化及本土化的做法就是当地设计、当地制造、当地销售以及当地融资、当地融智。

企业海外投资迥异于国内投资,前者的风险更大。成败因素取决于东道国政治、经济、文化和法律等各方面的影响。举例来说,一国的法律,如劳工、税收等,稍不留神,就可能因这样一个疏忽而使投资者蒙受巨大损失。这种事例在我国的海外投资中屡见不鲜,教训是深刻的。因此,我们必须认真研究东道国的法律法规,了解其经济政策以及有关商标注册和税收等方面的政策,严格遵守东道国的法律法规,依法经营,照章纳税,合理避税,不断提高产品质量和服务质量,积极稳妥地推进"本土化"战略。

Translation Skills (VI)

翻译中的虚实转换

语言是文化的载体,和文化相互依存,因此翻译不仅是两种不同语言的转换,也是两种不同文化的交融。由于英汉两种语言所涉文化的差异,对同一语义的英语表达可能笼统概括、抽象空泛,而汉语则形象生动、细腻具体,汉语可能抽象概括,而英语形象具体。具体或抽象的表达是英汉语言都具有的客观属性,而虚实互化的翻译方法则是基于这一客观属性上的一种技巧,也是英汉翻译中常见的技巧。所谓虚化实,即把抽象表达法转化为具体表达法,而实化虚即把具体形象的词进行概念化或抽象化处理。无论虚化实还是实化虚,都是为了实现翻译过程中的"达意",译者应在翻译时灵活巧妙地处理好原语与译语之间的虚实关系,以明白晓畅的译语再现原文主旨神韵。

一、虚化实

英语和汉语中有许多表达方法是抽象的,翻译时经常需要将这些抽象的表达作具体化引申,把抽象表达法转化为具体表达法,即虚表达化为实表达。

例1 China will be the largest economy in the world within 15 years.

译文:中国在15年内将成为世界上最大的经济体。

economy 直译成中文为"经济",汉语中"经济"表示抽象概念,如果该句直译成"中国在15年内将成为世界上最大的经济",显然不符合汉语的表达习惯。译文把表示抽象概念的词"经济"具体化为"经济体",不仅意思明确,也完全符合汉语表达习惯。

例2 Rich working experience was his entrée to this large international company.

译文:丰富的工作经验是他进入这家大型跨国公司的敲门砖。

entrée 是抽象名词,本意是"入场权;入场许可",此处将该词义具体引申为"敲门砖",使表达更加形象具体。

例3 There is more to their life than political and social and economic problems; more than transient everydayness.

译文:他们的生活远不止那些政治的、社会的和经济的问题,远不止一时的柴米油盐问题。

原句中,everydayness 原义为"日常性",词义很抽象,直译无法表达原句包含的具体意义,因此译文将其引申为词义具体的"柴米油盐问题",既符合汉语表达习惯,也揭示了原文意义。

例4 在他下乡之时,他教村民们学文化。

译文:During his stay in the countryside, he taught the villagers how to read and write.

"文化"本属上层建筑的范畴,抽象意味很浓,但是汉语中也经常用其表示比较小的范畴,如该句中即为"读书,写字"的意思,英译文将它翻译为 read and write,既具体形象,又忠实于原句意义。

例5 He is a valuable acquisition to the team.

译文:他是该球队不可多得的新队员。

英语句子中,acquisition 原义为"获得;获得物",词义比较概括抽象。翻译时,从这个句子的上下文中可看出,这里的"获得物"具体是指人,所以汉语译成"新队员"则具体明确。

例6 Each transaction is carried out in public and the information sent electronically to every brokerage office of the nation.

译文:每笔交易都是公开进行的,并通过电子设备将交易资料发往全国各地的每一家经纪行。

原句中,只用一个抽象的副词 electronically(电子地)就把通过电子设备发送交易信息这一具体做法表达出来,而汉语中必须将抽象表达化为具体表达才能准确传达原意。

二、实化虚

英汉互译时,常常会遇到某些词汇的意义很难处理,从词典中找不到适当的对应表达,若按原文直译,会使译文晦涩难懂,不能准确表达原文的意思,使人感到生硬别扭、莫名其妙。这时要从句子的语境或逻辑关系出发,将词义加以延伸或泛化,从原文相对的特定、具体延伸为译文的相对一般和抽象,从而使译文流畅自然。

例1 花园里面是人间乐园,有的是吃不完的<u>大米白面</u>,穿不完的<u>绫罗绸缎</u>,花不尽的<u>金银钱财</u>。

译文:The garden was a paradise on earth, with more <u>food</u> and <u>clothes</u> than could be consumed and more <u>money</u> than could be spent.

该句如果把"大米白面""绫罗绸缎""金银钱财"一一对应地直译出来,就显得刻板啰唆。如果透过字面意思,通过进一步的分析、理解将原文列出的具体东西进行归类总结,"大米白面"都是食物,"绫罗绸缎"全为衣物,"金银钱财"都指金钱,所以用英语 food, clothes 和 money 译出,既简洁明了,又不失原文含义。

例2 Alloy belongs to a <u>half-way house</u> between mixtures and compounds.

译文:合金是介于混合物和化合物之间的<u>中间物质</u>。

half-way 词典中解释为"半途的"或"中途的";house 意思是"房子""旅店"等,意义很具体。如果直译为"合金是介于混合物和化合物之间的中途旅店",不仅不通顺,也无法传达原意。这时,只有根据含义和上下文,将"中途旅店"抽象化引申,译为"中间物质"才能达意。

例3 我们都是来自<u>五湖四海</u>。

译文:We hail from <u>all corners of the country</u>.

汉语中的"五湖"和"四海"虽然是具体的表达,但却用来泛指范围之广,此时若将其直译为 five lakes 和 four seas,读者反而会感到莫名其妙,因此英译文最好从原文含义出发,虚译为 all corners of the country(全国各个角落)。

例4 Sam knows he can depend on his family, <u>rain or shine</u>.

译文:萨姆知道<u>无论境况如何</u>,他都可将家庭作为靠山。

rain or shine 字面意义为"无论下雨还是晴天",比喻"无论出现什么情况";由此可见,直译在汉语中转达的仅仅是字面意义,而非其在上下文中的比喻意义,因此只能根据上下文译为"无论情况如何"。

例5 那位老师异常了解孩子们的<u>喜怒哀乐</u>。

译文:The teacher had unusual insight into children's <u>emotions</u>.

汉语四字格"喜怒哀乐"生动具体地表达出了四种情感,但其实际所指是人类各种情感的总和,译成英语时根据译入语的表达习惯,只需 emotions 一词就能简洁明了地概括出汉语"喜怒哀乐"四字所要传达的意义。

总之,"虚化"译法和"实化"译法在文章的翻译中是辩证的统一体,英汉互译时无论采用"虚化"还是"实化"译法,都要具体情况具体分析,使用任何一种方法的目的都是使译文既忠实于原文又不拘泥于形式。需要虚化时就虚化,使句子变得灵活、概括;需要实化时就实化,使笼统的词、词组或句子变得形象具体,增强译文的鲜明性和可读性。

Translation Exercises

1. All disputes in connection with the Contract or the execution thereof shall be amicably settled through negotiation.
2. Inventories follow cash and receivables in order of liquidity.
3. Socialist market economy is a structure wherein public ownership plays a dominant role and various economic sectors enjoy common development.
4. Every part is individually checked before assembly.
5. 如果你们的报价有竞争力,我们准备大量订购男式衬衫。(competitive)
6. 他用存款购买股票和债券。(invest)
7. 那张票据上标明"不可转让"。(transferable)
8. 1975年后期,进口热开始了。(binge)

Passage A   (English-Chinese Translation)

Customizing Your China Wholly Foreign-Owned Enterprises
Chris Devonshire-Ellis

Words & Expressions

Work on the following words and expressions and write the translated version in the space provided:

telephone conference _____
emergency board meetings _____
expat manager _____
the term of office _____
the wholly foreign-owned enterprises _____
sales and marketing cost allocations _____
the National People's Congress _____
company management meetings _____
the articles of association _____
asset valuers _____
a liquidation scenario _____
prior to registration with the authorities _____

Board of Directors Article

We recommend keeping the board of directors small and allowing for board meetings to be held outside China or even by telephone conference. Emergency board meetings should be just that, "an emergency" and called at 24-hour notice, not one-month notice![1] Pay attention to the duties and responsibilities of directors.

General Manager Article

This is a legally responsible position so put it in the hands of someone you trust, ideally your expat manager in charge of production. Limit the term of office to a year to give you some leeway. General managers can be notoriously difficult to fire if employed under the long terms often used in standard articles.

Profits Repatriation Article

Can't find it in the basic draft? That's because it's not there. This needs to be built in, essentially giving your parent company the right to bill the wholly foreign-owned enterprises for services for management expertise, royalties, licensing agreements, interest on loans, research and development cost allocations, sales and marketing cost allocations and so on. If you don't have these drafted in, it becomes difficult to overlay the service contracts into the articles and obtain approval for this mechanism.[2] It could save you between 4 – 13 percent on your profit tax bill. Get it in there.

Trade Union Article

Again, standard clauses in the articles appear innocuous. However, if not dealt with and redrafted, these can lead to interference at the highest level in the way in which you operate your business.[3] This is additionally compounded by the fact that new regulations are due to be issued that strengthen the role and responsibilities of the labor union.

All companies in China have the right to form a "grass roots" labor union if there are at least 25 employees (including foreign workers). This structure is part of a massive national reporting and monitoring union that has its ultimate power base firmly within the National People's Congress, so this is a powerful organization.

If a union is formed, then the elected representative has the right to attend company management meetings, and the company must also fund the union with 2 percent of all employees' salaries each month (staff must also make a small contribution). Funds should be used for workers education, welfare and entertainment. Funds may also be used to provide legal support to employees with grievances against the company.

Restricting the union representative's access only to the portion of meetings during which staff and workers' right are to be discussed, while budgets for the use of union funds can also be agreed upon and implemented, can minimize management interference.[4]

So, some measures of control can be exercised via the articles of association as concerns the role of the labor union. However, we are still waiting confirmation of changes to their powers that may also need to be taken into account.

Merger and Acquisition Article

Again, not in basic drafts. So if you want to sell the business, how can you value it? It's easier to identify a set of rules beforehand. Identify asset valuers, accountants and industry professionals who can value the business. Make their decision final and binding with a time limit for offers to be accepted or bettered, and a mechanism for payment and share transfer itself.[5] You never know what will happen down the road, and who can tell what China or your business will be like in five years?

Liquidation Article

As mentioned earlier, try and link this to the production and profitability scales. Typically they are rather woolly in basic drafts, meaning interpretation can creep in and the local government, whose approval is required, may have different ideas as to what is and what is not a liquidation scenario, not least as they will want to maintain employment. The way to deal with this is to have the articles of association worded so as to link the termination clauses to production clause (this is not in standard drafts). In this way, an economic trigger is identified that can be pulled should the business underperform. This needs to be built into the articles of association prior to registration with the authorities. If approved, the licensing authority must follow its own approval process for the behavior of the company if it decides to exit for economic reasons.[6] It neatly puts the ability to exit back in the realms of measurable financial performance and away from any ambiguity.

Notes

[1] Emergency board meetings should be just that, "an emergency" and called at 24-hour notice, not one-month notice!

【译文】董事会的紧急会议应该是这样的,首先情况十分危急,其次必须是在会议前24小时通知,而不是会议前一个月通知。

【解析】这个句子看上去相当简单,但是翻译的时候却会感觉无从下手。主句很清晰,后半句讲述紧急会议的要求,an emergency 强调会议的紧急性,即"情况十分危急",called at 24-hour notice, not one-month notice 则是对会议的通知时间作出限制。相信通过这样讲解后,句子的翻译就迎刃而解了。

[2] If you don't have these drafted in, it becomes difficult to overlay the service contracts into the articles and obtain approval for this mechanism.

【译文】如果不将上述内容起草进公司章程,那么日后想要将这些服务合同补充进公司章程以及为这一机制获得批准将变得非常困难。

【解析】it becomes difficult to ... 中的 it 是形式主语,在翻译的时候,将真正主语"那么日后想要将这些服务合同补充进公司章程以及为这一机制获得批准"先译出。draft 意为"起草,草拟"。

overlay 意为"置(一物)于他物之上",这个意思在此显然不合适,根据前文"如果不将上述内容起草进公司章程",其逻辑意义应该是"后补"的意思,所以在此将其译为"补充进"。

[3] However, if not dealt with and redrafted, these can lead to interference at the highest level in the way in which you operate your business.

Business English Translation

【译文】然而,如果不对这些条款进行处理或重新起草的话,它们将会对经营企业的方式造成最大程度的干涉。

【解析】句中 at the highest level 用作 interference 的定语,意为"最大程度的"。

[4] Restricting the union representative's access only to the portion of meetings during which staff and workers' right are to be discussed, while budgets for the use of union funds can also be agreed upon and implemented, can minimize management interference.

【译文】只允许工会代表参加讨论职员和工人权利的会议,这样可以最大限度地减少对管理层的干涉;当然,供工会使用的资金预算也还是会得到批准并实施。

【解析】这句话的翻译关键在于 while budgets for the use of union funds can also be agreed upon and implemented 这句话的处理,译文中把该句放在最后,句意清晰明确。

[5] Make their decision final and binding with a time limit for offers to be accepted or bettered, and a mechanism for payment and share transfer itself.

【译文】要使他们的决定是最终的和有约束力的,决定中要包含接受或修改出价的时限以及支付和转让股份的机制。

【解析】final and binding 意为"最终的和有束缚力的",是契约用语。offer 是"报价,出价,报盘"的意思。句中 a time limit 和 a mechanism 是并列成分,这样句子的结构也就很明确了。

[6] If approved, the licensing authority must follow its own approval process for the behavior of the company if it decides to exit for economic reasons.

【译文】如果公司由于经济原因决定退出经营并且得到发证机关的批准,那么发证机关将按其审批程序对公司的退出经营行为进行审查。

【解析】licensing authority 是"发证机关";exit 是"退出"的意思,这里引申为"退出经营(活动)"。句中有两个 if 引导的条件状语从句,翻译时将它们合二为一,以使句子简洁明快。

Passage B (English-Chinese Translation)

Integrated Supply Chain Planning
Jeremy F. Shapiro

Words & Expressions

Work on the following words and expressions and write the translated version in the space provided:

integrated planning　　　　　　　　　　_____

intertemporal integration　　　　　　　_____

resource acquisition decisions　　　　_____

sustained competitive advantage　　　_____

efficient operations
capital investment decisions
product sales and gross revenues
a manufacturer of consumer durables
a wholesale grocery distributor
enhanced integration
confidential information

As we stated in the introduction, supply chain management refers to integrated planning. First, it is concerned with functional integration of purchasing, manufacturing, transportation, and warehousing activities. It also refers to spatial integration of these activities across geographically dispersed vendors, facilities, and markets. Finally, it refers to intertemporal integration of these activities over strategic, tactical, and operational planning horizons. [1] Roughly speaking, strategic planning involves resource acquisition decisions to be taken over long-term planning horizons, tactical planning involves resource allocation decisions over medium-term planning horizons, and operational planning involves decisions affecting the short-term execution of the company's business.

Intertemporal integration, which also is called hierarchical planning, requires consistency and coherence among overlapping supply chain decisions at the various levels of planning. [2] Although it is not yet widely appreciated, intertemporal integration is critical to the firm's sustained competitive advantage. Efficient operations will not lead to superior profits if the company's products are being manufactured in plants with outdated technologies that are poorly located relative to the company's vendors and its markets. Conversely, to evaluate a new or redesigned supply chain network, we must, at least approximately, optimize operations to be carried out under the design. [3]

Another aspect of intertemporal planning is the need to optimize a product's supply chain over its life cycle through the stages of design, introduction, growth, maturity, and retirement. Like most areas of strategic planning, life cycle planning requires integration of supply chain and demand management. For example, analysis of capital investment decisions in manufacturing equipment during the growth phase of a new product should take into account marketing decisions affecting product sales and gross revenues that may provide future returns sufficient to justify the investments. [4]

Improved integration of activities across multiple companies sharing components of a supply chain is a concern of increasing interest and importance. [5] Such integration is obviously relevant to the efficient operation of two companies after a merger or acquisition. It is also relevant to two companies that wish to tighten their working arrangements, such as a manufacturer of consumer durables and a major distributor of these durables or a manufacturer of food products and a wholesale grocery distributor. In such instances, integration is complicated because both companies have other vendors and customers; that is, their supply chains overlap significantly but are far from identical. Moreover, enhanced integration implies greater sharing of confidential information about costs and capacities as well as integrative management of business processes.

Developments in integrated supply chain planning have been both facilitated and required by advances in IT.[6] Managers today have much faster access to much more complete databases than they did only 5 years ago. The challenge is to transform this capability into competitive advantage.

Notes

[1] Finally, it refers to intertemporal integration of these activities over strategic, tactical, and operational planning horizons.

【译文】最后,它还指这些环节在战略、策略以及运营规划层面上的时际整合。

【解析】temporal 意为"时间的",与 spatial(空间的)相对应;intertemporal integration 译为"时际整合",比较符合上下文的意思。

[2] Intertemporal integration, which also is called hierarchical planning, requires consistency and coherence among overlapping supply chain decisions at the various levels of planning.

【译文】时际整合也叫作分级规划,它要求不同规划层面上重叠的供应链决策之间具有一致性和连贯性。

【解析】句中 which also is called hierarchical planning 是非限制性定语从句,直接按语序自然地译入句中即可。

[3] Conversely, to evaluate a new or redesigned supply chain network, we must, at least approximately, optimize operations to be carried out under the design.

【译文】相反地,为了评估新的或者是经过重新设计的供应链网络,我们必须优化经营,使其能按照设计的那样得以实施,至少大体上能做到。

【解析】这句话中的 at least approximately 是插入语,如果在句子中间翻译出来会使整个句子显得松散,因此译文中将这个插入语放在最后译出。

optimize 意为"优化",如 optimize the economic structure(优化经济结构), optimize the allocation of resources(优化资源配置)。

[4] For example, analysis of capital investment decisions in manufacturing equipment during the growth phase of a new product should take into account marketing decisions affecting product sales and gross revenues that may provide future returns sufficient to justify the investments.

【译文】比如说,在新产品成长阶段,对生产设备的资本投资决策进行分析时,应该考虑到影响产品销售和收入总额的营销决策,以便确定它是否能提供足够的未来回报来证明投资的合理性。

【解析】take into account 是"重视;考虑"的意思;gross revenue 意为"总收益,营业总收入";gross 意为"总的",比如 GDP(Gross Domestic Product 国内生产总值),GNP(Gross National Product 国民生产总值)。

本句采用了增译法来翻译 ... that may ... 这一部分,增加了表示目的的"以便……"这一结构,既符合上下文语境,也使整个句子意思更加流畅明了。

[5] Improved integration of activities across multiple companies sharing components of a supply chain is a concern of increasing interest and importance.

【译文】在多家共享供应链成分的公司中提高各环节的一体化水平,是人们日益关心,也是日渐重要的问题。

【解析】句中 sharing components of a supply chain 作 companies 的后置定语,但译成中文时按汉语表达习惯将其放在了先行词前面。

[6] Developments in integrated supply chain planning have been both facilitated and required by advances in IT.

【译文】信息技术的进步便利了,同时也要求一体化供应链规划的发展。

【解析】 原句是被动句,翻译时将其译成了主动句,这样符合汉语表达习惯。IT (=Information Technology)意为"信息技术"。

Passage C　(Chinese-English Translation)

中国企业融入国际采购链必须克服五大障碍

　　近年来,全球采购商在中国市场的采购活动日趋频繁,采购量持续上升。但有调查指出,中国供应商要实现与跨国企业的成功对接,还必须克服五大障碍:首先,中国企业由于担心泄密,往往不愿意提供各项财务报表、人力资源管理、生产流程管理资料等,或者将其"改头换面"之后才提供给采购商。一位长期在中国采购的跨国公司采购经理说,跨国公司如果愿意与某家供应商洽谈合作,要先签署保密协议,同时也要保证这些资料的准确性。然而,中方的不合作直接影响了双方的进一步合作。第二,重质量认证,轻实际操作。中国企业往往以为有了质量认证书就拿到了国际市场通行证。他们提供的产品样品质量很好,但在大批量供货时却总有大大小小的质量问题。第三,国内企业不愿意接受管理改造。通用电气(中国)公司的采购经理说,在全球采购中,采购商一旦选定了供应商,会将其当作自身的一部分,实施全方位的管理改造,确保这家供应商能够长期持续稳定地发展。然而,国内一些企业往往因为跨国公司提出对其管理进行全面改造时觉得麻烦而放弃了。第四,物流成本高。第五,企业社会责任意识淡薄。近年来,企业社会责任已经越来越多地出现在许多跨国公司订单的附加条件中。许多跨国采购商到中国企业考察时,先要查看职工食堂和厕所,了解企业如何保障职工身心健康、女职工的合法权益有没有得到有效保障等。

Translation Exercises

1. It was a pity that all Chinese football fans have not seen the spot final game on time.
2. Many divorced fathers only have access to their children at weekends.
3. Conversely, to be genuinely open, a society must be maintained with a fair and just rule of law along with strict discipline.

4. Her success had justified the faith her teachers had put in her.
5. 很遗憾我们在这一点上意见不一致。(agree on)
6. 改革使中国农村产业结构和就业结构不断得到优化。(optimize)
7. 评定他的表现时,不必考虑他的年龄。(take into account)
8. 新贸易协定应当会加快经济发展。(facilitate)

Passage A (English-Chinese Translation)

Industry Value Chain Analysis

Words & Expressions

Work on the following words and expressions and write the translated version in the space provided:

upstream and downstream	_____
in terms of the profit margin	_____
revenues and profits	_____
lease financing	_____
auto loans	_____
an area of primary expertise	_____
center of gravity	_____
core competencies	_____
vertical integration	_____
a consumer products company	_____

  The value chains of most industries can be split into two segments, upstream and downstream halves. In the petroleum industry, for example, upstream refers to oil exploration, drilling, and moving the crude oil to the refinery, and downstream refers to refining the oil plus the transporting and marketing of gasoline and refined oil to distributors and gas station retailers. Even though most large oil companies are completely integrated, they often vary in the amount of expertise they have at each part of the value chain.[1] Texaco, for example, has its greatest expertise downstream in marketing and retailing. Others, such as British Petroleum (now BP Amoco), are more dominant in upstream activities like exploration.

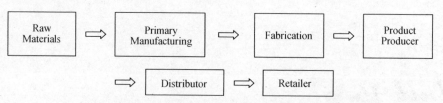

Figure 1 Typical Value Chain for a Manufactured Product

An industry can be analyzed in terms of the profit margin available at any point along the value chain. [2] For example, the US auto industry's revenues and profits are divided among many value chain activities, including manufacturing, new and used car sales, gasoline retailing, insurance, after-sales service and parts, and lease financing. From a revenue standpoint, auto manufacturers dominate the industry, accounting for almost 60% of total industry revenues. Profits are, however, a different matter. Auto leasing is the most profitable activity in the value chain, followed by insurance and auto loans. The core activities of manufacturing and distribution, however, earn significantly smaller shares of the total industry profits than they do of total revenues. [3] For example, since auto sales have become marginally profitable, dealerships are now emphasizing service and repair. As a result of various differences along the industry value chain, manufacturers have moved aggressively into auto financing. Ford, for example, generates nearly half its profits from financing, even though financing accounts for less than 20% of the company's revenues.

In analyzing the complete value chain of a product, note that even if a firm operates up and down the entire industry chain, it usually has an area of primary expertise where its primary activities lie. [4] A company's center of gravity is the part of the chain that is important to the company and the point where its greatest expertise and capabilities lie—its core competencies. According to Galbraith, a company's center of gravity is usually the point at which the company started. After a firm successfully establishes itself at this point by obtaining a competitive advantage, one of its first strategic moves is to move forward or backward along the value chain in order to reduce costs, guarantee access to key raw materials, or to guarantee distribution. [5] This process is called vertical integration.

In the paper industry, for example, Weyerhauser's center of gravity is in the raw materials and primary manufacturing parts of the value chain in Figure 1. Weyerhauser's expertise is in lumbering and pulp mills, which is where the company started. It integrated forward by using its wood pulp to make paper and boxes, but its greatest capability still lay in getting the greatest return from its lumbering activities. In contrast, Procter & Gamble is primarily a consumer products company that also owned timberland and operated pulp mills. Its expertise is in the product producer and marketer distributor parts of the Figure 1 value chain. P&G purchased these assets to guarantee access to the large quantities of wood pulp it needed to expand its disposable diaper, toilet tissue, and napkin products. P&G's strongest capabilities have always been in the downstream activities of product development, marketing, and brand management.

It has never been as efficient in upstream paper activities as Weyerhauser.[6] It had no real distinctive competence on that part of the value chain. When paper supplies became more plentiful (and competition got rougher), P&G gladly sold its land and mills to focus more on that part of the value chain where it could provide the greatest value at the lowest cost—creating and marketing innovative consumer products.

Notes

[1] Even though most large oil companies are completely integrated, they often vary in the amount of expertise they have at each part of the value chain.

【译文】即使多数大型石油公司都是完全一体化的,但是它们会在价值链的某一环节中所掌握的专门技术上有所差别。

【解析】value chain 意为"价值链",理论上这一概念是哈佛大学商学院教授迈克尔·波特于1985年提出的。波特认为,每一个企业都是在设计、生产、销售、发送和辅助其产品的过程中进行种种活动的集合体。所有这些活动可以用一个价值链来表明。

[2] An industry can be analyzed in terms of the profit margin available at any point along the value chain.

【译文】研究一个产业可以从整个价值链的任何一点可获得的利润幅度着手。

【解析】in terms of 意为"根据;从……方面(来说)",如:

It has been a terrible year in terms of business.

就生意而论,这是很糟糕的一年。

We generally measure the value of material goods in terms of money.

我们通常用金钱计量有形物的价值。

any 用于肯定句,意为"任何";profit margin 意为"利润率;利润幅度"。

[3] The core activities of manufacturing and distribution, however, earn significantly smaller shares of the total industry profits than they do of total revenues.

【译文】然而,生产和分销之类的核心经营活动所赚取的利润在整个产业利润中所占的份额远远少于它们在总收入中所占的份额。

【解析】翻译这句话时,关键是要分析句子的结构。句中出现了比较复杂的比较级,比较的核心词是 shares(份额),比较的对象是"核心经营活动所赚取的利润在整个产业利润中所占的份额"和"核心经营活动所赚取的利润在总收入中所占的份额"。弄清了句子的结构后,翻译的难题也就迎刃而解了。

[4] In analyzing the complete value chain of a product, note that even if a firm operates up and down the entire industry chain, it usually has an area of primary expertise where its primary activities lie.

【译文】在分析一个产品的整个价值链时,值得注意的是:即使一家公司可以全面地管理经营整个产业链,它也通常会有一个特别擅长的领域,这也就是其主要经营活动所在。

【解析】up and down 本义是"上上下下,前前后后,来来往往",但在这句话中译为"全面"更合理;an area of primary expertise 意为"主要专门技能区域",实际可引申为

"特别擅长的领域"。

[5] After a firm successfully establishes itself at this point by obtaining a competitive advantage, one of its first strategic moves is to move forward or backward along the value chain in order to reduce costs, guarantee access to key raw materials, or to guarantee distribution.

【译文】一家公司通过获得竞争优势而成功地在这一点上确立了自己的地位后,它的早期战略步骤之一就是在价值链中向上游企业或下游企业拓展,以减少成本、保证获得主要的原材料以及确保分销渠道畅通。

【解析】competitive advantage 意为"竞争优势";move forward or backward 本义是"向前移动或向后移动",但是这样的译文放到句中很生硬而且不易理解,结合上下文得知供应链有上下游关联企业,因此这里将其译成"向上游企业拓展或向下游企业拓展",这样就很容易理解了。

[6] It has never been as efficient in upstream paper activities as Weyerhauser.

【译文】宝洁公司在上游纸业经营活动中从来没有像惠安纸业公司那样有效。

【解析】这里 it 指宝洁公司,根据上下文得知,宝洁公司在拓展下游经营活动方面很有能力,而惠安纸业公司在拓展上游经营活动方面做得很好,掌握了正确信息,翻译这句话时就容易了。

Passage B (English-Chinese Translation)

Outsourcing: Growth by Building on Existing Business

Words & Expressions

Work on the following words and expressions and write the translated version in the space provided:

conceive the idea of doing sth. _____

comparable proportion _____

system integration _____

seat-making plants _____

satellite plants _____

a standardized business operating system _____

the design work _____

individual customers _____

an Internet-based database _____

real-time status updates _____

existing customers _____

leading supplier of integrated facility management _____

In the early 1980s, Johnson Controls was known for heating controls and plastic containers, not for automotive products. Until 1985 automobile manufacturers made car seats in their own factories, and it was then that Johnson and another company, Lear, conceived the idea of supplying those essential parts of a car's interior for them. [1]

Now the company estimates that 80 percent of the seating in American-made cars is outsourced, while in Europe the comparable proportion is 70 percent. According to the company, demand from automakers for a single supplier of seating systems is expected to grow "due to opportunities system integration creates for cost reduction, parts consolidation, weight reduction, quality and safety improvements, enhanced functionality, and vehicle differentiation". [2] As Johnson's customers move overseas, they expect Johnson to supply them from local facilities. In response, the company has established over 130 seat-making plants, most of which are in the United States and Europe. Many are satellite plants located close to big car factories, to which the seats are delivered straight to the assembly line as needed. To manage the complexity of a global production system, the company is creating a standardized business operating system and a single, global infrastructure, thus helping to eliminate variation and inefficiencies across factories. [3]

Johnson is striving to increase the input of its engineers to the design work so that it can use the results in the seats of other car manufacturers. "Three years ago, 80 percent of our development work was done on behalf of individual customers and only 20 percent was our own proprietary designs," says Johnson's president. "Today the proportion is about 60∶40 and our goal is to turn this to 20∶80." In 1999, the company launched an Internet-based database that employees worldwide can use to post and retrieve factory-tested best practices and ideas for improving performance in such areas as quality, cost, timelines, productivity, and morale of employees. [4] Another private website allows the company's suppliers to provide real-time status updates, generates progress reports, and helps program managers quickly identify problems.

Another strategy has been to expand its role from supplying seating to include nonseating areas of car interiors (roof interiors and trim). This is part of a move to supply a "total interior" service to automakers. [5] A further step in this direction is the introduction of a satellite-based communications system built into a car's interior.

Johnson Controls, building on the knowledge that its existing customers are its largest source of growth, has expanded its outsourcing to include the operation and maintenance of commercial buildings full-time for customers for which it once was the source for just heating and ventilation controls. [6] It is now the world's leading supplier of integrated facility management, with a portfolio of over 1.2 billion square feet of building space in 35 nations.

Notes

[1] Until 1985 automobile manufacturers made car seats in their own factories, and it was then that Johnson and another company, Lear, conceived the idea of supplying those essential parts of a car's interior for them.

【译文】直到1985年,汽车制造商一直都是在自己的工厂里生产汽车座椅,也就是在这个时候,美国江森自控公司和另一家公司力尔公司才开始构思向那些制造商供应汽车内部的基本配件。

【解析】it is ... that ... 是一个强调句结构,被强调部分通常放在 that 前面,如:
It was the quality of the product that appealed to me.
吸引我的是产品质量。
Johnson Controls 和 Lear 两家公司都是生产汽车内部配件的公司。

[2] According to the company, demand from automakers for a single supplier of seating systems is expected to grow "due to opportunities system integration creates for cost reduction, parts consolidation, weight reduction, quality and safety improvements, enhanced functionality, and vehicle differentiation".

【译文】据公司所说,美国汽车制造商对于单个的座椅设备系统供应商的需求有望增加,这是由系统一体化为降低成本、合并零部件(生产)、降低重量、改善质量与安全、提高汽车性能以及实现车辆差异化所提供的机遇引起的。

【解析】句中 cost reduction, parts consolidation, weight reduction, quality and safety improvements, enhanced functionality, and vehicle differentiation 都是名词短语,但翻译时都采用动宾结构以保证全句的通顺。

[3] To manage the complexity of a global production system, the company is creating a standardized business operating system and a single, global infrastructure, thus helping to eliminate variation and inefficiencies across factories.

【译文】为了应对全球生产系统的复杂局面,公司创造了一个标准化的企业运营体系和一个单独的、全球性的基础设施,以帮助消除工厂之间的差异和无效性。

【解析】句中包含两个状语 to manage the complexity of a global production system 和 thus helping to eliminate variation and inefficiencies across factories,中间是独立的主句,翻译时按照原句结构直接译出即可。

[4] In 1999, the company launched an Internet-based database that employees worldwide can use to post and retrieve factory-tested best practices and ideas for improving performance in such areas as quality, cost, timelines, productivity, and morale of employees.

【译文】1999年,公司建立了基于因特网的数据库,这样全球职工都可以使用它来公布或检索经工厂检验过的最佳做法与想法,从而改善诸如质量、成本、时序、生产力以及职工斗志等方面的工作情况。

【解析】retrieve 本义是"寻回;恢复;补救",在该句中译为"检索(储存的信息)"。
翻译本句之前,要先理清句子结构,主句是 the company launched an Internet-

based database,后面的部分则是一个较长的定语从句。

[5] This is part of a move to supply a "total interior" service to automakers.

【译文】这是迈向给汽车制造商提供"全套内饰"服务行动中的一部分。

【解析】total 意为"全体的,全部的",如 total quality management(全面质量管理)。全面质量管理是指充分发挥每一雇员作用使其为企业创造最大效益的一种管理学理论。

[6] Johnson Controls, building on the knowledge that its existing customers are its largest source of growth, has expanded its outsourcing to include the operation and maintenance of commercial buildings full-time for customers for which it once was the source for heating and ventilation controls.

【译文】美国江森自控公司知道现有的顾客就是它最大的成长源泉,它现在已经将其外包扩大到专职向顾客提供商业建筑的运营与维护,而对于这些顾客而言,这家公司曾经只是加热装置和通风设备的供应商。

【解析】building on the knowledge that its existing customers are its largest source of growth 是状语,意为"基于它现有的顾客就是它最大的成长源泉这一认识",如将其放入句中读来拗口,所以翻译时进行了适当调整,将这一状语译成了谓语,从而使全句语义清晰、表达流畅。

Passage C (Chinese-English Translation)

什么是服务外包?

服务外包产业是现代高端服务业的重要组成部分,具有信息技术承载度高、附加值大、资源消耗低、环境污染少、吸纳就业(特别是大学生就业)能力强、国际化水平高等特点。当前,以服务外包、服务贸易以及高端制造业和技术研发环节转移为主要特征的新一轮世界产业结构调整正在兴起,为我国发展面向国际市场的现代服务业带来了新的机遇。牢牢把握这一历史机遇,大力承接国际(离岸)服务外包业务,有利于转变对外贸易增长方式,扩大知识密集型服务产品出口;有利于优化外商投资结构,提高利用外资的质量和水平。

外包是指企业将价值链的某些环节交给外部企业去完成的一种商业措施,是被国际企业特别是跨国企业普遍采用的战略手段,是全球范围内社会化分工协作的高端形式。外包,按地域可分为"境内外包"和"离岸外包";按发包形式,可分为"项目外包"和"职能外包";按业务范围,可分为"制造外包"(蓝领外包)和"服务外包"(白领外包)。服务外包,主要分为信息技术外包(ITO)和业务流程外包(BPO)。ITO 的主要业务范围有:IT 系统操作服务、IT 系统应用管理服务和 IT 技术支持管理服务,包括软件外包等。BPO 业务范围包括:需求管理,如管理企业与客户之间关系;企业内部管理,如人力资源、财务管理;供应链管理,如采购、仓储、运输;业务运作管理,如呼叫中心、客户咨询、金融信用。相对于传统的 ITO 而言,BPO 是当今服务外包发展的主要形式并呈渐强趋势。

Translation Skills（Ⅶ）

否定句的翻译

英语的否定形式是一个常见而又比较复杂的问题,否定形式的使用非常灵活、微妙,被认为是英语的一大特点。在表达否定概念时,英语在用词、语法和逻辑等方面都与汉语有很大不同。有的英语句子形式上是肯定的而实质上是否定的,有的则形式上是否定的而实质上是肯定的。英语否定词否定的范围和重点有时难以判断,否定词在句子中有特殊的表示强调的方法,某些否定词和词组的习惯用法较难掌握。此外,英汉两种语言在表达否定意义的方式和手段上存在着的差异也是不容忽略的。汉语习惯于重复使用同一种否定词来表达否定的意义,而英语,尤其在书面语言中,则避免重复同一否定词来表达否定意义。因此,在翻译英语否定形式时必须细心揣摩,根据上下文来分析考虑,正确判断英语否定句中否定词的否定范围或焦点,真正彻底地理解其含义及否定的重点,然后根据汉语的习惯进行翻译。我们在平时的学习中还应该了解英美人的思维方式,不断总结归纳出英语中有关否定的习惯表达法,才能正确地理解英语的否定句,准确地处理好译文。

英语和汉语的否定句都可以分成完全否定、部分否定和双重否定。

完全否定就是对全句的否定,英语常用的完全否定词与习惯用语有:no,not,none,nobody,nothing,nowhere,neither,nor,not at all 等,把具有完全否定意义的英语句子翻译成中文时,一般把否定词照翻即可。

部分否定则是对 some,all,both,every,many,much,always,often 等词的否定,此时不论否定词"not"放在这些词的前面,还是与句中谓语一起构成否定式谓语,该句都属于部分否定。

双重否定则是两个否定词并用,否定同一个单词,或者一个否定词否定另一个否定词,其否定意义互相抵消而得到肯定意义。英语的双重否定的类型主要有以下三种:否定词＋含否定词缀(un-,in-,dis-,non-,nor-,no-,-less 等)的表示否定意义的词;否定词＋without＋(动)名词;否定词＋含蓄否定词或某些有保留的否定词,其中含蓄否定词是指形式上肯定,意义上否定的词或词组,如 refuse,neglect,fail,lack,stop,protect ... from ...,keep(prevent)... from ... 等,有保留的否定词则是指并非一概否定而又起强调语气的词,如 but,until,except,unless,too 等。对于双重否定句的翻译,能直译的尽量直译,当然当直译并不能很好地表达原文的意思,那么也可以选择肯定译法。

下面我们讲述几种固定的特殊的否定表达。

例 1 The number of people who consult psychiatrists today is not, as is sometimes felt, a symptom of increasing mental ill health.

译文:今天这么多人去找精神病医生咨询,并不像人们常常所感觉到的那样说明精神病患者的数目正在日益增多。

对于"not ... as ＋从句/like＋短语"这种否定句的翻译,我们所遵循的原则是:"as ＋从句"或"like 短语"位于否定词 not 之后,则处于 not 的否定范围内,并且"as ＋从句"或"like 短语"要用肯定式,不能再用任何否定词。但是,如果把"as ＋从句"或"like 短语"放在句首,成了否定句的外位语,它们就在 not 的否定范围之外了。

例 2 The greatness of a people is no more determined by their number than the greatness of a man is determined by his height.

译文：正如一个人的伟大不取决于他的身高一样，一个民族的伟大也不取决于其人口多少。

在"no more ... than + 从句/not ... any more than + 从句"的结构中，否定词不但否定 than 前面的内容，也否定 than 后面的内容。事实上，than 前面的内容和它后面的内容是同等意义上的否定句，且两者构成某种意义上的类比。因此，than 后面的从句只能用肯定式，不能用任何否定词。

在此顺便谈谈两对否定短语 no more than 与 not more than，no less than 与 not less than 的译法。not more than 相当于 at most（至多），而 no more than 相当于 only（只有）；而 not less than 可译为"不下于""至少""不比……差"，no less than 译为"达……之多""和……一样"。

例 3　The film is not instructive and interesting.

译文：这部影片颇有教育意义，但是没有趣味。

有人会把上句理解为"这部影片既无教育意义，又没有趣味"。如果把原句中的 and 改为 or，那么这种译文是对的。我们在翻译这种句子的时候要注意：当 and 在 ... not ... and ... 结构中连接两个状语（或定语，或表语）的时候，与之搭配的 not 表示部分否定，即只否定 and 后面的部分。

最后，将具有否定意义的常见词汇列举如下：

动词：lose，scorn，lack，outlive，outgrow，ignore，neglect，refuse，deny，miss 等；名词：absence，failure，denial，refusal，lack，exclusion，omission，ignorance，neglect，loss，draw（不分胜负）等；形容词：bad，doubtful，little，few，foreign（无关的），strange，missing，ignorant，short of，free from，far from，blind to 等；副词：in for（免不了），in the air（悬而未决），at large，in the rough（未成熟）等；介词：above，before，beyond，under，within，beneath，past，but，without，except，instead of，in place of，out of，anything but 等；连词：unless，until，or，lest，rather than，much more，still less，let alone 等。

Translation Exercises

1. American presidents tend to be judged less by the good deeds they set in motion than by how well they respond to crises.
2. Looking at the picture, I couldn't help missing my middle school days.
3. This forces management of both international and domestic companies to search for ways to lower costs while improving their products to remain competitive.
4. Commonly, outsourcing firms provide key components of data processing, logistics, human relations, and accounting, although any activity in the value chain can be outsourced.
5. 我们必须建立起良好的商业信誉，以拓展我们的业务。（build on）
6. 暂不发货，听候指示。（not ... until）
7. 在那个周末因高速驾驶造成的交通事故很多。（due to）
8. 他试图从文件中检索地址。（retrieve）

Unit 17

Passage A (English-Chinese Translation)

Electronic B2B in the Auto Industry

Words & Expressions

Work on the following words and expressions and write the translated version in the space provided:

conduct transactions	_____
commercial markets	_____
transact business at great distances	_____
drive up rather than reduce their own costs	_____
novel proposal	_____
foreign affiliates	_____
strategic partners	_____
self-contained	_____
global electronic market	_____
ordering costs	_____

  As we observed in the text, a market is a mechanism for exchange between the buyers and sellers of a particular good or service. [1] In earlier times, markets were actual physical settings where buyers and sellers would gather to conduct transactions. While such market settings are still used for selling things such as fish, fruits and vegetables, and antiques and collectibles, many commercial markets today differ in a fundamental respect: Buyers and sellers do not actually meet at the same place, but rather arrange their exchanges via mail orders, telephones, fax machines, and so forth. The growth of the Internet is making it even easier for some buyers and sellers to transact business at great distances. [2]

  A good example of this trend is the recently announced partnership among some of the world's largest automobile manufacturers. It all started when various individual automakers began to create their own global purchasing websites. [3] Ford Motor Co., for instance, planned a site it called Auto-Xchange. The company intended to post all of its global procurement needs on the site, while also requesting that its suppliers post availability and prices for parts and equipment.[4]

When it became apparent that other automakers were planning to do the same thing, major suppliers to the auto industry realized that they might soon be facing an unwieldy array of separate websites for each car company—a situation that would potentially drive up rather than reduce their own costs. Thus a coalition of the largest suppliers approached Ford and General Motors with a novel proposal: Why not team up and create a single site that could be used by both automakers and by their suppliers?[5]

Ford and GM executives quickly saw the wisdom of this idea and then convinced DaimlerChrysler to join them. Now the Big Three plan to establish a single website to serve as a marketplace for all interested automobile manufacturers, suppliers, and dealers—essentially, a global virtual market including all firms in the industry. Almost immediately, France's Renault and Japan's Nissan, which is controlled by Renault, indicated a desire to join; Toyota also indicated strong interest. In addition, both Ford and GM indicated that they would encourage their foreign affiliates and strategic partners as well. The partners who are building the website intend to establish it as a self-contained organization that will eventually offer shares to the public.[6]

Many experts believe that the impact of this global electronic market will be tremendous. It currently costs GM about $100 in ordering costs to buy parts or supplies the traditional way—with paper or over the telephone. However, the firm estimates that its ordering costs will drop to less than $10 under the new system. Clearly, the automakers will realize substantial cost savings. Suppliers, too, will benefit in various ways. Besides having more information about the immediate needs of different customers, they will be able to buy and sell among themselves.

Notes

[1]　As we observed in the text, a market is a mechanism for exchange between the buyers and sellers of a particular good or service.

【译文】从课文中我们得知,市场是买卖双方进行特定商品或服务交易的机构。

【解析】mechanism 有"机械装置""途经,手法""机制,机构"等多种含义,这里取"机构"之义比较合适。

exchange 这里是"交易,交换"的意思,该词在商务英语中还表示"兑换率",如:

What is the rate of exchange between the dollar and the pound?

美元和英镑之间的兑换率是多少?

此外,exchange 还有"交易所"的意思,如:

Most big cities have stock exchanges—the New York Stock Exchange being the best known.

多数大城市都有证券交易所,其中最著名的是纽约证券交易所。

[2] The growth of the Internet is making it even easier for some buyers and sellers to transact business at great distances.

【译文】因特网的迅速发展使得买卖双方进行远程交易变得更加便捷。

【解析】transact 是"处理,办理"的意思,一般情况下 transact business 可以直接翻译成"交易",而不必死译成"处理业务";transact 的名词形式为 transaction,意为"交易,业务",如:

In view of the small amount of this transaction, we are prepared to accept payment by D/P as requested.

鉴于这笔交易金额不大,我们准备按你方要求以付款交单方式接受付款。

[3] It all started when various individual automakers began to create their own global purchasing websites.

【译文】这一切都始于各类个体汽车制造商开始创建自己的全球采购网站。

[4] The company intended to post all of its global procurement needs on the site, while also requesting that its suppliers post availability and prices for parts and equipment.

【译文】公司打算把其全球所有采购需求公布在网站上,并要求供应商将零部件和设备的有无和价格也公布出来。

【解析】动词 procure 是"努力取得,获得"的意思,如:

A friend procured a position in the bank for my brother.

一位朋友为我的兄弟在银行里谋得了一个职位。

该句中 its global procurement needs 是指"公司在全球(对零部件和设备)的采购需求"。

[5] Thus a coalition of the largest suppliers approached Ford and General Motors with a novel proposal: Why not team up and create a single site that could be used by both automakers and by their suppliers?

【译文】因此,最大的几家供应商联合起来与福特和通用进行接洽并提出一个新颖的建议:为什么不合作建立一个汽车制造商和供应商共用的网站?

【解析】approach 这里是"与……接洽"的意思;novel 这里作为形容词,意思是"新颖的,新奇的";team up 意思是"合作",如:

They teamed up with another company to develop new products.

他们与另一家公司合作开发新产品。

[6] The partners who are building the website intend to establish it as a self-contained organization that will eventually offer shares to the public.

【译文】正在建立网站的合伙人打算将其建成一个能够最终向公众出售股份的独立机构。

【解析】self-contained 意为"独立自主的;门户独立的",所以这里将 self-contained organization 译为"独立机构"。

句中 offer shares to the public 译为"向公众出售股份",offer 除了有"提供,拿出"的意思,还可以表示"出价,报盘;备有……出售",如:

They offered twenty thousand pounds for the shop.

他们出价两万英镑,要求收购这个铺子。

Passage B (English-Chinese Translation)

Profit Is No Object

Words & Expressions

Work on the following words and expressions and write the translated version in the space provided:

e-commerce explosion _____
dot.com businesses _____
seasoned investors _____
gambling speculators _____
brand-name manufacturers _____
core operation _____
highly respected mutual fund manager _____
go through the roof _____
influx of investment capital _____
weak financial controls _____
extravagant advertising _____
promote products at below-cost prices _____
a team of independent auditors _____

One of most well-publicized aspects of the e-commerce explosion has been the enormous wealth created for owners of, and early investors in, such dot.com businesses as America Online, Amazon.com, and eBay.com. In many cases, these businesses have not yet earned any profits, and for some profitability is still years off, at best. But amid the smoke and thunder of the Internet explosion, seasoned investors and gambling speculators alike have been willing to bet big sums of money on the prospect of even bigger paydays. [1] While there may be many beneficiaries of these investments, business founders are typically at the top of the list. But as the e-commerce craze appears to be settling down, the boards of directors of some of these firms are increasingly taking a closer look at what is going on.

Consider, for example, the case of Craig Winn and Value America, Inc. Winn is an ambitious entrepreneur whose resume includes one business bankruptcy and virtually no experience in technology or technology management. Nevertheless, he successfully launched Value America on July 4, 1996, with a 250-page business plan and a personal investment of $150,000. The mission of Value America was to serve as a distribution pipeline between manufacturers and consumers across a wide array of product lines, effectively eliminating traditional wholesalers and retailers altogether. [2]

Winn believed that consumers would order any of tens of thousands of products from over 1,000 different brand-name manufacturers—everything from caviar and laundry detergent to gas barbecue grills and home computers. Value America would transmit the order directly to the manufacturer, who would fill the order and send it directly to the consumer. From a business standpoint, the beauty of Winn's plan was that the firm would not carry any of its own inventory. [3] Rather, it would simply serve as a communication conduit with little of its own capital tied up in anything but its core operation.

Almost immediately, investors began hopping onboard. When the first big investment came in ($10 million from the Union Labor Life Insurance Co.), Winn quickly paid himself back his own $150,000, claiming that it had been a business loan all along, and set his own salary at $295,000 a year. Soon, more and more money began pouring in including major investments by Paul Allen, one of the cofounders of Microsoft, and Fred Smith, founder and CEO of Fed Ex.

Winn also stocked Value America's board of directors with big-name investors and dignitaries, giving both him and his start-up instant credibility to complement his stockpile of cash. [4] Prominent board members included Smith, former cabinet member William Bennett, former Newell-Rubbermaid vice-chairman Wolfgang Schmitt, and highly respected mutual fund manager Bill Savoy. Value America's IPO took place on April 8, 1999, and its share price went through the roof, opening at $23 a share and reaching a first day high of $74.35 before settling at $55. This influx of investment capital gave the profitless three-year-old firm a market value of $2.4 billion and made Winn rich overnight.

Unfortunately, the hole in the roof created by the soaring stock price uncovered some fundamental flaws at Value America—problems that eventually forced the board to take serious action. For example, major cost overruns, weak financial controls, extravagant advertising, and alleged mismanagement by Winn began to undermine the firm's effectiveness even as its stock price was still rising. [5] Winn had ordered a plush corporate jet even as the firm's losses were mounting, personally ordered the printing and mailing of a 1999 Christmas catalog despite the fact that it was weeks too late, and heavily promoted products at below-cost prices.

Finally, on November 23, 1999, the board ousted Winn as chairman and brought in a new professional management team to shore up the struggling enterprise. [6] At that point, Winn, still a member of the board, began dumping his stock. Between November 24, 1999, and April 6, 2000, he sold almost $36 million worth of it. Combined with earlier stock sales, this brought his personal gain to a stunning $53.7 million. Meanwhile, the new management team was frantically cutting costs and laying off employees in hopes of saving the company. But another major blow came on March 30, 2000, when a team of independent auditors expressed doubts that the firm could survive as a going concern. And

Winn? He was enjoying the majestic views from his new mansion on a 150-acre estate in Virginia.

Notes

[1] But amid the smoke and thunder of the Internet explosion, seasoned investors and gambling speculators alike have been willing to bet big sums of money on the prospect of even bigger paydays.

【译文】在因特网爆炸散发出的滚滚硝烟和隆隆雷声中,经验丰富的投资者和具有冒险精神的投机者们都很乐于把大笔资金赌在可能给他们带来更多收益的事业上。

【解析】payday 意为"发薪日;(喻)大发利市的日子",这里如果将 the propect of even bigger payday 直译出来,会显得很别扭,所以采用意译法将其译出。

[2] The mission of Value America was to serve as a distribution pipeline between manufacturers and consumers across a wide array of product lines, effectively eliminating traditional wholesalers and retailers altogether.

【译文】Value America 的使命就是作为生产商和消费者之间的一个分销渠道,跨过多重生产线将产品从生产商处分销到客户手中,同时有效地将传统批发商和零售商淘汰出局。

【解析】distribution 在商务英语中是"分配;销售"的意思,distribution channel 或 distribution pipeline 都是指"分销渠道"。eliminate 本意是"消除,排除",这里如果直译成"排除传统的批发商和零售商",不但句子不通顺,意思也不明确,所以意译成"将传统批发商和零售商淘汰出局",用"淘汰出局"明确传递了 eliminate 包含的意义。

[3] From a business standpoint, the beauty of Winn's plan was that the firm would not carry any of its own inventory.

【译文】从商业的角度来看,Winn 的计划高明之处在于公司不会有任何库存积压。

【解析】beauty of Winn's plan 这里被意译为"Winn 的计划高明之处",因为汉语里形容一个计划不会用"美丽",通常用"高明"。inventory 是"存货"的意思,如 merchandise inventory 指"商品库存"。

[4] Winn also stocked Value America's board of directors with big-name investors and dignitaries, giving both him and his start-up instant credibility to complement his stockpile of cash.

【译文】Winn 邀请许多社会知名的投资者和显要人物加入 Value America 的董事会,使他本人和刚起步的公司立即信誉大增,并借此实现现金的积累。

【解析】big-name investors and dignitaries 意为"知名投资者和显要人物"。start-up 本意是"启动",从上下文中可以得知,这里的 start-up 表示"刚起步的公司"。stockpile 意思是"积蓄,贮存",所以 stockpile of cash 译成"现金的积累"。

[5] For example, major cost overruns, weak financial controls, extravagant advertising, and alleged mismanagement by Winn began to undermine the firm's effectiveness even as its stock price was still rising.

【译文】尽管股票价格还在上涨,但是主要成本超支、财务监管不力、广告铺张浪费以及

Winn 的管理不善开始削弱公司的运作效力。

[6] Finally, on November 23, 1999, the board ousted Winn as chairman and brought in a new professional management team to shore up the struggling enterprise.

【译文】1999 年 11 月 23 日,董事会最终免去了 Winn 的主席职务,并引进一支新的专业管理团队来挽救步履维艰的企业。

【解析】oust 是"免某人(职),罢黜"的意思。shore up 意思是"支撑,支持",为了使表达更加贴切,shore up the struggling enterprise 这里译作"挽救步履维艰的企业"。

Passage C (Chinese-English Translation)

C2C 电子商务

随着经济的全球化发展,网络经济正在很大程度上改变着人们的生产和生活方式。电子商务以其快捷、开放、超越时空限制等特性给经营者带来了巨大商机,同时也给消费者带来了空前的便利。

C2C 电子商务模式是消费者对消费者的电子商务模式,其特点就是消费者与消费者讨价还价进行交易。C2C 网站的本意则是构建一个网上二手跳蚤市场,个人将其闲置物品发布到网上供其他有需要者购买,而非从盈利角度来专门出售商品。

然而,现在的 C2C 电子商务模式实际上已经是一种纯商业行为。C2C 商家与现实中的个体户其实没有区别。不同的是,个体户必须在国家工商行政管理部门登记注册并取得营业资格后才能在经许可的经营范围内营业。而网上开店不需要经过任何行政审批过程,只需在 C2C 网站上注册用户,提交身份证复印件即可。因此,网上开店的商家就不必像那些工商个体户那样去纳税,同时由于网上开店不需要像实体店那样缴纳租金等原因,吸引了越来越多实体商店的商家将其部分或全部生意转移到 C2C 网站去经营。这一问题已经引起了国家有关方面的注意,相信迟早会得到合理解决。

Translation Exercises

1. The transaction is a simple exchange of long-term debt for shares of stock.
2. As soon as we have received your inquiry, we will immediately mail you the samples and offer you most favourable prices.
3. The Latin American Free Trade Association seeks gradually to eliminate trade barriers among its members.
4. Merchandise inventory is the quantity of goods on hand and available for sale at any given time.
5. 尽管我们做了最大的努力,但连一个递价都没有弄到。(procure)
6. 他的交易大多是在电话上做的。(transact)
7. 那两个公司已合作研制新型赛车。(team up)
8. 他用该证据来支持自己的论点。(shore up)

Passage A　(English-Chinese Translation)

Inspiring Wine Games
Inesa Pleskacheuskaya

Words & Expressions

Work on the following words and expressions and write the translated version in the space provided:

moderate tippling　　　　　　　　　　　　　　　_____
finest works　　　　　　　　　　　　　　　　　　_____
a good few cups of wine　　　　　　　　　　　　　_____
masters of painting and calligraphy　　　　　　　　_____
the Saint of Calligraphy　　　　　　　　　　　　　_____
flowing cup　　　　　　　　　　　　　　　　　　_____
take their inspiration from the wine　　　　　　　　_____
suit all social and literary tastes　　　　　　　　　_____
fling out one's hands　　　　　　　　　　　　　　_____

　　Liquor was originally a main feature of ancient ceremonial rites in China. As to drinking habits, Chinese people regard moderate tippling as good for the health. There is a tradition of soaking traditional Chinese medicine in liquor in order to achieve a better effect, and its success in this respect has been proved.[1] Alcohol has also been the preferred remedy for keeping out the cold for thousands of years.

　　In imperial times, alcoholic beverages had direct connections with the military, as it was believed that a drop of drink brought courage, invigorated the weary and heightened army morale.[2] During the Warring States Period (476 – 221 BC), Qin Mugong of the Qin State poured alcoholic mash into the Yellow River, which he and his soldiers then proceeded to drink and get merry on. In historical novels, alcohol, battles and skullduggery are frequently connected. *The Romance of Three Kingdoms* describes how Guan Yu chopped Hua Xiong's head off while his wine was still warm and how Zhang Fei, pretending to be drunk, captured his enemy's fortress with ease. Alcohol features in almost every chapter of this classic novel.

The drink had even greater impact on Chinese artists, since many produced their finest works while under the influence. Many famous poets, such as Li Bai and Du Fu, wrote their finest works after a good few cups of wine. This was also the case for masters of painting and calligraphy. Famous calligrapher Wang Xizhi, known as the Saint of Calligraphy, finished his most outstanding work, *Lantingxu* (*The Orchid Pavilion Prologue*) while drunk. After sobering up he tried several times to improve on this piece of work executed while in his cups, but failed.[3] The tablet bearing *Lantingxu* has pride of place in the Orchid Pavilion near Shaoxing City, Zhejiang Province, considered a sacred site by Chinese calligraphers. One of the most popular entertainments at the pavilion echoes that enjoyed by bygone poets and calligraphers—that of the "flowing cup". Players sit on opposite banks of a narrow stream on which flat-bottomed cups are placed to float along with the flow. When a cup stops in front of someone on the bank, they must drink the wine and recite a poem. In former times, poets were expected to create a poem on the spot, and so literally took their inspiration from the wine. The world-famous Shaoxing rice wine is, therefore, the source of many great poetic works.

There are also other, less refined, drinking games or *jiuling*.[4]

Jiuling goes back to the Western Zhou Dynasty (1046 – 771 BC). It was intended to restrict drinking and ensure observation of rules of etiquette. There were, and still are, many forms of *jiuling* to suit all social and literary tastes. They fall into three broad categories of general, competitive and literary.

Everybody can play the general games, which includes jokes, riddling and *chuanhua*, which means passing the flower. This kind of *jiuling* is often played during "ladies only" banquets. Another name for *chuanhua* is the "Gong Show", whereby when someone behind a screen or another unseen place beats a drum or gong the people sitting around the table begin quickly passing around a flower. When the gong stops, whoever is holding the flower must take a drink and perform a song, recite a poem or tell a story.

Competitive *jiuling* consists of archery, arrow pitching, chess playing, dicing, finger guessing and animal betting. Finger guessing is played by two players who both fling out their right hands, showing a few fingers while simultaneously calling out a number from nil to ten. If the fingers showing on the hands of both players add up to one of the numbers called, the caller wins and the loser must take a drink. To make the game more exciting, players give names to the numbers they call, in a way similar to bingo, for example saying "two kind brothers" for two, "three stars shining" for three, and "making a fortune in four seasons" for four and so on. There are, as may be expected, regional variations.[5]

"Animal betting" involves players tapping one another's chopsticks while simultaneously calling out: stick, tiger, rooster or insect. The rules are simple: stick beats tiger, tiger eats rooster, rooster pecks insect, and insect bores stick.

These two games are known to everyone in China and are much enjoyed. But people with a good education and knowledge of the traditional culture—intellectuals as they were once known—consider such games vulgar. They play a more specialized version that requires a broad literary knowledge and quick wits. [6] It is similar to the games famous poets and artists of the past played. Names of animals are substituted for fine literary fragments, such as quotations from Buddhist sutras, history, poems, proverbs, and fairy tales. Such games are consequently enlightening and intellectually stimulating. China's great poet Bai Juyi said once that literary *jiuling* is more entertaining than chamber music. Anyone for fine wine and poetry?

Notes

[1] There is a tradition of soaking traditional Chinese medicine in liquor in order to achieve a better effect, and its success in this respect has been proved.

【译文】有一种传统是把中药浸泡在酒中以寻求更好的药效,在这方面的成功也获得了证实。

【解析】traditional Chinese medicine 是专业术语,简写为 TCM,译为"中药",也有人用 Chinese herbal medicine 来指中药。

in this respect 是"在这个方面"的意思,相关词组有 in respect of/to(关于;就……而言;在……方面),如:

It's going to raise a lot of problems in respect of atmosphere pollution.

这将在大气污染方面引起诸多问题。

In respect to your request, fifty dollars is being credited to your account.

就你所要求之事,将 50 美元记入你账户的贷方。

[2] In imperial times, alcoholic beverages had direct connections with the military, as it was believed that a drop of drink brought courage, invigorated the weary and heightened army morale.

【译文】在帝王时代,酒类饮料与军队有直接的联系,人们相信微量的酒能带来勇气、鼓舞疲倦的士兵、加强军队的斗志。

【解析】it was believed that … 译为"我们相信……",正如 it was said that … 可以翻译成 "据说……,他们说……";后面的三个动宾短语的翻译只要在保证结构一致的前提下直译就行了。

[3] After sobering up he tried several times to improve on this piece of work executed while in his cups, but failed.

【译文】他酒醒之后,试了好几次想对他喝醉时成就的这一作品进行润色,但是他没能成功。

【解析】sober up 意思是"清醒起来";in one's cups 意思是"喝醉的";fail 是具有否定意义的词,在这里译成"没有成功",更能达到句子所要表达的效果。

[4] There are also other, less refined, drinking games or *jiuling*.

【译文】还有其他不太优雅精致的饮酒游戏或酒令。

【解析】refined 意思是"优雅的;精致的",less refined 则译成"不太优雅精致的",而不需要译出其具体的比较对象。

[5] There are, as may be expected, regional variations.

【译文】正如可以预料到的那样,酒令是会有地区差异的。

【解析】as may be expected 译为"正如可以预料到的那样";在翻译 there be 句型的时候,可以视情况的不同加上主语或保持原句结构,如在 Note [4] 中没有添加主语,而这一句中则添加了主语"酒令"。

[6] They play a more specialized version that requires a broad literary knowledge and quick wits.

【译文】他们所玩的游戏是更专业性的,需要广泛的文学知识和敏捷的思维。

Passage B (English-Chinese Translation)

China's Changing Cityscapes

Words & Expressions

Work on the following words and expressions and write the translated version in the space provided:

be dressed up as sites for visiting tourists

denote specific religions

break away from convention

saintly scriptures and relics

the twin Small and Large Wild Goose pagodas in Xi'an

drum towers and wind-and-rain bridges

space-age architecture

incorporate Oriental characteristics with dazzling results

be imbued with a rich architectural heritage

under threat of annihilation

The vision of China as a country full of architecture topped with upswept roofs, built around walled courtyards, connected to gardens full of tranquil lotus ponds by zigzag bridges is a little antiquated in the 21st century.[1] While open-sided pavilions, temples and pagodas, moon gates and the like can still be found throughout China, such traditional edifices are now generally dressed up as sites for visiting tourists. Traditional temple and palace buildings typically feature circular columns linked by beams and a curved roofline with upturned eaves and ceramic tiles. From the 8th century on the eaves, featuring colorful sculpted animals and figures, became increasingly decorative.

In the south of China curves and ornamentation were more exaggerated, as in Guangdong's Foshan Ancestral Temple. Columns were carved in stone or painted with different colors denoting specific religions (bright red for Buddhists, black for Taoists), or the rank of palace occupants. Four-sided roofs, higher platforms or special yellow-glazed roof tiles, might distinguish imperial buildings. [2] Occasionally, buildings broke away from convention in unique style, such as the circular-tiered buildings of the Temple of Heaven in Beijing. Like most important buildings in China, the temple was raised above ground level and built on a stone platform. Despite the oddity of that design, building materials and ground plans for traditional architecture have been strictly adhered to for countless generations.

Pagodas were originally introduced from India with Buddhism and intended to house saintly scriptures and relics, but were often used to guard cities. Most have a central stairway rising through an uneven number of storeys. Some survive from the Tang Dynasty—like the twin Small and Large Wild Goose pagodas in Xi'an. As evidence of days when marauding bandits were the norm, defensive walls can still be found around some settlements. A 14-kilometer Ming Dynasty city wall still encircles the center of Xi'an and smaller rural walled villages can still be found, even in Hong Kong. Efforts are being made to recover and renovate parts of old city walls in many Chinese cities including Beijing and Nanjing. [3]

Extremes of climate in the north spawned solidly insulated brick walls, while sub-tropical southern temperatures encouraged the use of open eaves, internal courtyards and wooden lattice screens. In the mountains of Guizhou and Guangxi, the Dong and Miao minorities still build large cedar wood houses, as well as drum towers and wind-and-rain bridges without nails. In Yunnan, Lijiang boasts hundreds of wooden homes and classic Dai minority houses, to the south in Xishuangbanna, are built on stilts. Patches of traditional wooden architecture survive in other cities including Kunming and Chengdu.

The remnants of past architectural triumph are now, more often than not, dwarfed by adjoining modern day skyscrapers soaring into the sky. [4] China has enthusiastically embraced space-age architecture as a statement of its future ambition. The works of the world's most renowned architects, including I. M. Pei, John Portman, Michael Graves, Norman Foster, Richard Rogers, Paul Andreu and Jean-Marie Charpentier, are integral features of China's new cityscapes. The Jinmao Building in Shanghai, designed by Skidmore, Owings and Merrill and the tallest in China, demonstrates how an international look can incorporate Oriental characteristics with dazzling results. Its cavernous atrium, parts of the highest hotel in the world-spirals spectacularly upwards over 33 floors. However space-age buildings may become, though, the traditional Chinese consideration *of fengshui* generally remains very important. [5]

On the east coast, remnants of European and Japanese colonial architecture give the former treaty ports a very distinctive look. Shanghai paraded styles of architecture from all over the world in the 1930s. On the Shanghai Bund, the Zhongshan Circle in Dalian and the Qingdao waterfront, steel-and-glass skyscrapers vividly offset the former neo-classical and art deco splendor.

The past and present collide in many Chinese cities imbued with a rich architectural heritage, as the demands of modernization and property speculation take precedence. [6] Whilst some of the grander buildings may escape the bulldozer, huge tracts of housing embodying the quintessential character of cities like Beijing and Shanghai have been razed. In Beijing the traditional *siheyuan* or four-sided courtyard dwellings, set in mazes of small lanes, or *hutongs*, are under threat of annihilation. In Shanghai the very distinctive *shikumen* or stone-framed door dwellings, a British-style terrace with Chinese characteristics, face a similar fate.

Notes

[1] The vision of China as a country full of architecture topped with upswept roofs, built around walled courtyards, connected to gardens full of tranquil lotus ponds by zigzag bridges is a little antiquated in the 21st century.

【译文】有人把中国想成是充满这样一种建筑的国家:向上微翘的屋檐,由围墙环绕成的一个个庭院,蜿蜒的小桥连接着满是宁静莲花池的花园。这种想法在21世纪已经过时了。

【解析】翻译这句话时,先确定主句,即The vision is a little antiquated,然后再将其余成分根据汉语习惯逐一译出。

[2] Four-sided roofs, higher platforms or special yellow-glazed roof tiles, might distinguish imperial buildings.

【译文】四面坡顶、高楼台以及特有的黄釉屋顶瓦片都是帝王宫殿的特征。

【解析】distinguish意思是"辨别,区别;为某人(某事物)的特征或特性",翻译时将其由动词转换为名词意义,这样译文就比较通顺。

[3] Efforts are being made to recover and renovate parts of old city walls in many Chinese cities including Beijing and Nanjing.

【译文】在中国的许多城市,比如北京、南京,人们都在努力恢复和修补古老的城墙。

【解析】Efforts are being made to ... 是make efforts的被动语态,相似的句型还有:pay attention to ... 的被动语态是attention be paid to ... 。

[4] The remnants of past architectural triumph are now, more often than not, dwarfed by adjoining modern day skyscrapers soaring into the sky.

【译文】过去辉煌建筑物的遗迹如今在周边高耸云霄的现代摩天大楼的映衬下往往显得十分矮小。

【解析】past architectural triumph 可以译成"过去建筑上的重大成就",但是加上 remnants,则很难合理搭配,因此将其译为"过去辉煌建筑物的遗迹";more often than not 相当于 frequently,意为"往往"。

[5] However space-age buildings may become, though, the traditional Chinese consideration of *fengshui* generally remains very important.

【译文】然而无论(现代)建筑物如何具有太空时代的特征,中国传统上对于风水的考虑仍然是非常重要的。

【解析】space-age 意为"太空时代的";副词 though 用在句子中间,前后用逗号隔开,意为"可是,然而"。

[6] The past and present collide in many Chinese cities imbued with a rich architectural heritage, as the demands of modernization and property speculation take precedence.

【译文】随着现代化和房地产投机需求的日益重要,在许多充满丰富建筑遗产的中国城市中古代建筑和现代建筑相互抵触。

【解析】be imbued with 意为"充满";take precedence (over) 意为"优于……;(地位或程度上)高于……",如:
Control of prices takes precedence over every other consideration.
控制物价比其他问题都更应优先考虑。

Passage C (Chinese-English Translation)

古老而年轻的苏州

中华民族文化,自古博大精深,源远流长。孕育于长江下游和太湖流域的吴地文化,则是其中一个重要的组成部分。

苏州地处长江三角洲腹地,位于中国沿海经济开放带与长江经济发展带之交汇处,山明水秀,物华天宝,历来就是吴地文化的精华所在。几千年悠久的历史给苏州留下了迷人的人文古迹。各级文物保护单位,数量众多,保存完好。

苏州历代文人辈出,自古被誉为"文荟之邦"。著名的政治家、思想家、文学家、艺术家、科学家不胜枚举,昆剧、评弹、苏剧、古代建筑等都具有较高的历史和文化地位。吴门书画、篆刻等流派纷繁,各呈千秋,形成了具有独特魅力的吴文化。

苏州气候宜人,温婉秀丽。"君到姑苏见,人家尽枕河",这是唐代诗人对水城苏州的形象描绘。作为中国最著名的风景旅游城市之一,闻名遐迩的苏州园林,无疑是一朵绚丽多姿的艺术奇葩。著名的拙政园、网师园、留园、环秀山庄已被联合国列入《世界遗产名录》。咫尺天涯,山水交融,集自然美、建筑美、绘画美为一体。近年来,苏州古典园林还出口海外,首开先例的如美国大都会博物馆中的"明轩",即仿造明代风格的网师园,该园于1988年荣获国际特别成果奖,这更使得苏州这座古城名扬四海。

"上有天堂,下有苏杭",苏州不仅风光旖旎,还是江南著名的"鱼米之乡"。境内土地肥沃,物产丰富。著名的太湖四珍、阳澄湖大闸蟹、碧螺春茶叶、洞庭红橘等远近闻名;酒店、宾馆、饭店鳞次栉比,各具特色。

[名城苏州]解说词

Translation Skills（Ⅸ）

数字的翻译

在商务英语的翻译中,很多领域都会涉及数字的翻译,其中包括数字的总数、数字的变化和变化幅度以及数字的倍数等。由于数字在英语和汉语中表达的方式不同,数字的翻译对于很多学生来说无疑是一大难点。

1. 数字的表达

数字在英语和汉语中的表达方式是不同的。汉语是个、十、百、千、万、十万、百万、千万、亿、十亿……,也就是以"十"的倍数来表示；而英语则是在数字超过千以后,以"千"（thousand）的倍数来表达,如"一万"是"十千",即 ten thousand；"十万"是"百千",即 hundred thousand；"百万"为 million。百万以上的数字则用"百万"的倍数表达,如"千万"是"十百万",即 ten million；"亿"是"百百万",即 hundred million；"十亿"为 billion。对于四位以上的数字,我们也可以说汉语中是四位计数（万,亿）,而英语中是三位计数（thousand, million, billion, trillion）。了解了两者的区别之后,我们在翻译数字的时候就要注意思维和表达方式的转换。

翻译时常会遇到一些较笼统的数字,如"几个""十几个""几十个"等,这类表达法需要熟记:几个（some, a few, several, a number of）,十几个（more than ten, no more than twenty）,几十个（dozens of）,几十年（decades）,七十好几（well over seventy）,好几百个（hundreds of）,成千上万（thousands of）,几十万（hundreds of thousands of）,亿万（hundreds of millions of）等。

例1 123456789

在英语中,我们这样看:123,456,789,读作:one hundred and twenty-three million four hundred and fifty-six thousand seven hundred and eighty-nine。

在汉语中,我们这样看:1,2345,6789,读作:一亿两千三百四十五万六千七百八十九。

2. 数字倍数的表达以及翻译

英语表示倍数增减或倍数对比的句型多种多样,其中有一些很容易译错,主要原因在于:英汉两种语言在表述或对比倍数方面存在着语言与思维差异。现将常用的英语倍数句型及其正确译法归纳如下:

A is n times bigger (longer, more …) than B.

A is n times as big (long, much …) as B.

A is n times the size(length, amount …)of B.

以上三句都表示 A 的大小（长度,数量……）是 B 的 n 倍或 A 比 B 大（长,多……）n－1 倍。

increase to n times

increase n times/n-fold

increase by n times

increase by a factor of n

以上四式都表示:增加到 n 倍(或增加 n−1 倍)。

例 2　The production of this factory has been increased to three times as compared with that of last year.

译文:这家工厂的产量比去年增加了 2 倍(增加到去年的 3 倍)。

在这类句型中 increase 常被 raise,grow,go/step up,multiply 等词所替代;同样,表示倍数减少可用 decrease,reduce,shorten,go/slow down 等。在翻译倍数减少的句子时,要注意 decrease by 3 times 应译为"减少 2/3",而不是"减少 3/4"。

例 3　Switching time of the new-type transistor is shortened 3 times.

译文:新型晶体管的开关时间缩短了 1/3(即缩短到 2/3)。

英语中还有表示倍数的专用词汇:double(增加 1 倍),treble(增加 2 倍),quadruple(增加 3 倍)。

例 4　China's annual income per capita of 2004 quadrupled that of 1994.

译文:2004 年中国的人均年收入比 1994 年翻了两番(比 1994 年增加了 3 倍)。

Translation Exercises

1. It used to be believed that the earth is the center of the universe.
2. There will be another bridge across the Yellow River with the quick development of the economy of China.
3. Every effort is being made by local clubs to interest more young people.
4. She had to learn that her wishes did not take precedence over other people's needs.
5. 她的声音里充满着一种不寻常的严肃语气。(be imbued with)
6. 事情正如我们预料的那样发生了。(as ... expected)
7. 雾大时火车往往会误点。(more often than not)
8. 明辨是非当然要紧。(distinguish)

Bibliography

Aaker, David A. *Strategic Market Management* [M]. 6th ed. New York: John Wiley & Sons, Inc., 2001.

Ball, Donald A., et al. *International Business: The Challenge of Global Competition* [M]. 8th ed. New York: McGraw-Hill/Irwin, 2002.

Bernstein, Peter L. & Damodaran, Aswath. *Investment Management* [M]. New York: John Wiley & Sons Inc., 1998.

Devonshire-Ellis, Chris. Customizing your china wholly foreign-owned enterprises [J]. *Beijing Review*, 29 March 2007: 40.

Faber, Marc. Catching market waves [N]. *Time*, 26 June 2006.

Faber, Marc. Wealth on the wing [N]. *Time*, 24 April 2006.

Griffin, Ricky W. & Ebert, Ronald J. *Business* [M]. 6th ed. London: Pearson Education Limited, 2002.

Li, Jian. Industrial Park leads Suzhou's eastward development [N]. *China Daily*, 6 January 2006.

Madura, Jeff. *International Financial Management* [M]. 6th ed. Cincinnati: South-western College Publishing, 2000.

Pleskacheuskaya, Inesa. Inspiring wine games [J]. *China Today*, October 2006: 42.

Roach, Stephen. Risk adjusted [N]. *Time*, 31 July 2006.

Rugman, Alan M. & Hodgeetts, Richard M. *International Business: A Strategic Management Approach* [M]. London: Pearson Education Limited, 2000.

Samuel, J. Mantel Jr., et al. *Project Management in Practice* [M]. New York: John Wiley & Sons. Inc., 2001.

Shapiro, Jeremy F. *Modeling the Supply Chain* [M]. USA: Wadsworth Group, 2001.

Solomon, Michael R. *Consumer Behavior* [M]. 5th ed. Upper Saddle River: Prentice-Hall, Inc., 2002.

Storey, John. Managing innovation [A]. In Craine, Stuart & Dearlove, Des (eds), *Financial Times Handbook of Management* [C]. London: Pearson Education Limited, 2001: 616-618.

Wheelen, Thomas L. & Hunger, J. David. *Strategic Management and Business Policy* [M]. 8th ed. London: Pearson Education Limited, Inc., 2002.

程极明. 世界经济与政治格局中的焦点[A]. 江苏对外经济贸论坛,2006 (3): 63.

段瑞春. 自主品牌:市场的直接交锋[N]. 苏州日报,2007 – 03 – 07.

金国钧. 浅谈我国海外企业的生存与发展之道[A]. 江苏对外经贸论坛,2006(1):99.

金焕荣. 文化差异——跨国公司必须逾越的障碍[J]. 苏州大学学报(哲学社会科学版),2001(2).

那复祺. 通胀与调控[N]. 国际金融报,2004 – 05 – 21.

那复祺. 投机——让人欲罢不能[N]. 国际金融报,2004 – 04 – 02.

祁崇兆. 浅谈企业人才管理问题[A]. 江苏对外经贸论坛,2006(2):91.

施用海. 循环经济:实现外贸增长方式转变的战略选择[A]. 江苏对外经贸论坛,2006(1):54.

王 艳. 论我国"专门比较优势"的存在与转化[J]. 对外经贸实务,2007(4):21.

魏秀敏. 国际金融服务外包的运作模式及其启示[J]. 对外经贸实务,2007(2):57.

张忠如. 谈人民币汇率改革与国际收支、外汇储备和外债[A]. 江苏对外经贸论坛,2006(2):87.

周欢怀. C2C电子商务模式下的税收问题[J]. 对外经贸实务,2007(3):55.